082772

D0715159

Walks from Llandudno

Christopher Draper

ISBN: 0-86381-559-6

Cover design: Alan Jones

First published in 1999 by
Gwasg Carreg Gwalch, 12 Iard yr Orsaf, Llanrwst, Wales LL26 0EH
℡ 01492 642031   📠 01492 641502
📧 books@carreg-gwalch.co.uk   Internet: www.carreg-gwalch.co.uk

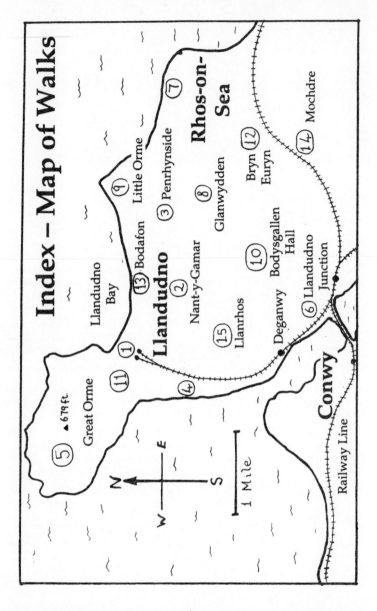

Index – Map of Walks

- Great Orme ▲ 679 ft.
- ⑤
- ⑪
- ④
- ①
- Llandudno Bay
- Llandudno
- ⑬ Bodafon
- Little Orme
- ⑨
- ⑦
- Rhos-on-Sea
- ③ Penrhynside
- Nant-y-Gamar
- ②
- Glanwydden
- ⑧
- ⑮ Llanrhos
- ⑩
- Bodysgallen Hall
- Bryn Euryn
- ⑫
- ⑭ Mochdre
- Deganwy
- ⑥ Llandudno Junction
- Conwy
- Railway Line

N ←
W — S
E

1 Mile

Contents

Introduction

Every part of the landscape has a story to tell. This book unlocks some of the stories of the farms and castles, shops and quarries, lanes and byways that surround Llandudno. You will find some walks to be more scenically satisfying than others because I have tried to select walks that cover a variety of aspects of local history. A derelict factory or abandoned quarry may not be as attractive as a Victorian seafront, but all form an essential part of the Llandudno Story. The result is a varied mix of pastoral rambles, marine strolls and town trails.

The Llandudno area contained a number of different settlements before the advent of tourism, and I have incorporated explorations of the hinterland as well as the town centre. The area covered by this book very roughly corresponds with an area known for hundreds of years as *Creuddyn*. However I have strayed over administrative boundaries, both ancient and modern, in order to provide walks that are conveniently centred on Llandudno.

These are walks for strollers and ramblers rather than athletes and mountaineers, and any reasonably fit person should have no problem completing them. Some are along paved surfaces, but the field paths are always liable to get a little muddy and overgrown. Waterproof shoes or boots are always a good idea, and shorts are often a bad idea. A waterproof jacket is also handy but no special equipment is required. The maps and directions should enable you to navigate fairly easily, but an ordnance survey map would increase your enjoyment and understanding of the overall geography of the area. All of these walks are conveniently covered by the Pathfinder 736 map.

The practical details are clearly set out at the start of each walk – description, and where a walk does not begin from the centre of Llandudno I have given public transport details. The trains, trams and buses are part of Llandudno's history and using them, rather than private transport, obviously helps maintain them and protect that fascinating environment we seek to explore.

Walking is hungry work and I have therefore included details of a suitable refreshment stop on every route. I have tried to select pubs and cafés that fit the historical context of each walk, as well as providing reasonably priced, wholesome food and drink. If you include such relaxed refreshment and reflection stops you could easily devote half a day or more to each walk.

It is a good idea to read the whole of the relevant chapter before setting out on a walk as it helps to set the historical framework, and avoids any route-finding errors. Some readers may prefer to remain armchair walkers, rambling around the routes in their imagination; but by walking a path, you help maintain our precious ancient rights of access to the countryside and to our shared history.

Happy walking.

Christopher Draper

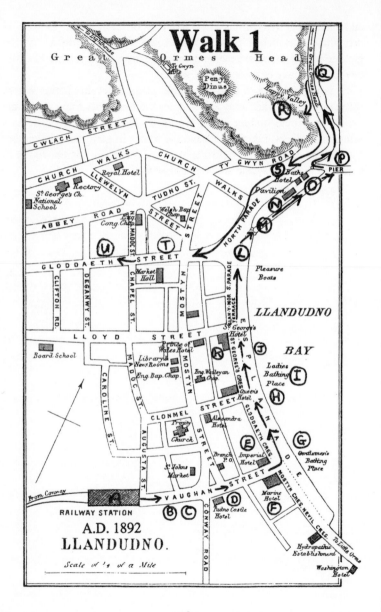

Walk 1

G r e a t   O r m e s   H e a d

Ty Gwyn Mill

Pen y Dinas

Ty Gwyn Road

Happy Valley

To Lighthouse
to Lighthouse

To Great Ormes Head

GWLACH STREET

CHURCH WALKS

CHURCH STREET

CHURCH WALKS

Royal Hotel

LLEWELYN

Rectory

St George's Ch.

National School

ABBEY ROAD

TUDNO ST.

STREET

Eng. Cong. Chap.

MADOC ST.

Welsh Bap. Chap.

Bath Hotel

Pavilion

PIER

GLODDAETH STREET

Market Hall

CHAPEL ST.

NELSON ST.

NORTH PARADE

Pleasure Boats

LLANDUDNO

CLIFTON RD.

DEGANWY ST.

LLOYD STREET

Board School

MADOC ST.

Prince of Wales Hotel

Library & News Rooms

Eng. Bap. Chap.

Eng. Wesleyan Chap.

MOSTYN STREET

LLAN-Y-MOR S. PARADE TERRACE

St George's Hotel

ST GEORGE'S CRES.

BAY

E S P L A N A D E

Ladies Bathing Place

CAROLINE ST.

MADOC ST.

CLONMEL STREET

Trinity Church

AUGUSTA ST.

Queen's Hotel

MOSTYN STREET

GLODDAETH CRES.

Alexandra Hotel

Branch P.O.

Imperial Hotel

St Johns Market

Gentlemen's Bathing Place

From Conway

RAILWAY STATION

VAUGHAN STREET

CONWAY ROAD

Rudno Castle Hotel

Marine Hotel

MOSTYN CRES. NEVIL CRES.

To Little Orme

Hydropathic Establishment

Washington Hotel

A.D. 1892
LLANDUDNO.

Scale of ¼ of a Mile

10

A Genial and Delightful Resort

Walk Number: One
Distance: Two miles
Terrain: Very easy, mainly along the promenade
Start: Llandudno railway station, Vaughan Street
Finish: The Clarence Hotel, Gloddaeth Street
Transport: Central

Introduction:

As the Victorian era comfortably slipped into the Edwardian age, Llandudno was a wonderful and lively, yet elegant, town. Tourists came here by land and by sea. This walk introduces us to the town as it might have been seen by a holiday-maker strolling from railway carriage to lunch, by way of the prom and the pier. Welcome to a Genial and Delightful Resort.

The Walk and Points of Interest:

A. The present station building dates from 1891, when it replaced the earlier 1858 building which could no longer accommodate the number of visitors. (If you look carefully you can still identify some remaining fragments of the original station: at the platform-edges the earlier, lower levels are exposed; some early advertising has been partly revealed by the removal of a later wall on the far right.) The new station needed all of its five platforms to cope with the trains, which arrived every few minutes in the summer season.

Carriages would await arrivals on the long carriageway situated between platforms two and three.

1. Walk from the station (A) down Vaughan Street; pause outside the gallery (B). The Post Office (C) is next door.

B. Oriel Mostyn was officially opened by Lady Augusta Mostyn in 1902, as the Mostyn Art Gallery. It initially concentrated on exhibiting the work of the Gwynedd Art Society, but soon widened the range of its displays. A 1904 newspaper report enthused over an exhibition that included tapestry work, oriental tiles and jewellery, as well as figurative and commemorative painting. The report concluded, 'Rarely have I seen in any town in Wales such a choice little collection of pictures'. The gallery served as a drill hall during the First World War, and was then used for a variety of commercial functions until it was reopened as a gallery in 1978.

C. The impressive Post Office building was opened on Friday 20th May, 1904 by the Postmaster General, Lord Stanley. The menu of the celebratory 'Déjeuner' included 'Lobster Salad, Galantine of Turkey, Truffled Lamb Cutlets in Aspic, Ox Tongue and Meringue Tart'. This was the Golden Age of the picture postcard, when few people had either cameras to record holiday memories, or telephones to receive holiday messages.

2. Continue to the Tudno Castle Hotel (D).

D. I can do no better than introduce The Tudno Castle in the words of a newspaper article of 1892:

> . . . This hotel is so conveniently situated just halfway from station to shore that it may be said to be within touch of both . . . built in the year 1862 the necessity for increased accommodation has resulted in the extension and alteration of the premises, culminating in the fine building now in existence . . . On the right of the hall is a cosy reading and writing room, the walls of which exhibit some capital oil paintings . . . The billiard room is a favourite resort, in fact one of the most popular in town, and contains a solid and beautiful Ashcroft improved cushion table . . . There are two splendid bathrooms in the establishment . . . The Van Gruisen piano cost the proprietors upwards of 130 guineas . . . Last year Mr Ernest Benzon, better known as the 'Jubilee Plunger'

stayed here for many months . . . The Tudno Castle has always been a prime favourite as a locale for dinner; for instance the Tradesmen's Dinner is generally held here . . .

3. Continue and cross to the promenade; look back at the Imperial Hotel (E), and the Marine Hotel to your right. If you turn to face the beach and the sea, you will be looking at the spot marked G on your map.

E. The Imperial Hotel was originally made up of separate guest houses that were united under single ownership and management in 1872. During the Second World War it became the headquarters of Britain's Inland Revenue Department.

F. The Marine Hotel made a unique contribution to the history of Llandudno for in 1890 it was, for five weeks, the home of the Queen of Romania. She took the same short route to the Marine from the station, where she had arrived in the Prince of Wales' own silk upholstered railway carriage. Strange as it might seem, her visit made a huge impact on the town. Crowds of up to six thousand people turned out to see her, wherever she went. A firework display was organised, a commemorative medal was struck, and streets were named in her honour. When she finally departed a salute of twenty-one lifeboat rockets was fired from the Great Orme. The great irony is that she only came by mistake. She had requested a recuperative holiday to be arranged somewhere remote, and to her agents in London, what could seem more remote than a distant town in Wales? She was horrified to arrive at a popular, lively holiday resort when she had needed a contemplative retreat. The friendship and adulation she received, and the picturesque setting of the town, seem to have quickly won over her affections. Her parting words, describing Wales as a haven of peace and beauty remain, translated into Welsh, as Llandudno's official motto, *Hardd, Hafan, Hedd.*

G. If you had stood on this spot in August 1909 you would have witnessed some of the good citizens of Llandudno giving an altogether less appreciative reception to another well known female visitor, Miss Mary Gawthorpe. Mary Gawthorpe was a leading suffragette and socialist, and she had come to support local activists in their campaign to secure Votes For Women. The suffrage cause had been established in Llandudno at a meeting in the Cocoa House on 23rd January 1907, and Llandudno soon became the centre of campaigning in North Wales. No sooner had Mary started addressing public meetings on the beach than the Council prohibited her from continuing. The suffragettes ignored the council and meetings continued here, opposite the Marine Hotel. The Llandudno Advertiser reported that groups of men continued to interrupt the speakers, and kept bursting into noisy renditions of popular music hall songs like, 'Has anybody here seen Kelly?' and 'Oh, Antonia' (sic). The Advertiser, however, was much impressed by Mary Gawthorpe and her fellow speakers, describing them as fluent and humorous and invariably scoring off the rowdies with their witty retorts.

4. Walk along the prom towards the pier, until you are opposite the Queen's Hotel (H),

H. The Queen's Hotel opened in 1855 and the unusual post-box outside is almost as old. It dates from 1865 and is of the rare Penfold design,

where you can also ponder the arrangements for sea bathing in Queen Victoria's days (I).

I. For centuries local people had bathed and swam as and when they wished, sensibly removing their clothes first. This scandalised English visitors to the infant bathing resort, and the town's Improvement Commissioners decided that such spontaneous, uncontrolled behaviour was bad for business, and they had better step in and control matters. The first move, in 1855, was to segregate the sexes. From the Imperial Hotel eastwards towards the Hydro was reserved for gentlemen. Ladies were permitted to bathe between St George's Hotel and the Queen's Hotel. This left a one hundred and fifty stretch of no-man's,

TUDNO CASTLE
HOTEL,
LLANDUDNO.

This newly established Hotel is pleasantly situated at the entrance to the Town, and commands extensive views of sea and mountain.

THE COFFEE ROOM,

Which is spacious, is equally available for Ladies as Gentlemen.

A Pleasant Drawing Room

Is also set apart for the use of Visitors.

TABLE D'HOTE
At 5-30.

An Excellent Billiard Table.

HOT, COLD, AND SHOWER BATHS,

Arrangements made for Winter Board.

TERMS SENT ON APPLICATION,

M. LOGAN, Proprietress.

or woman's, land in between. Matters were not fully resolved because ladies staying at hotels overlooking the gentlemen's bathing area were often embarrassed by gentlemen who emerged from their bathing machines wearing neither the apron or drawers supplied. Further regulations were introduced and the full, or *'University'*, bathing suit was gradually adopted, and in 1894 Llandudno went as far as to allow mixed bathing. Not wishing to move too quickly with the times, the bathing machines were not immediately abandoned, and they did not disappear completely from Llandudno beaches until 1958.

J. The bandstand, though attractive, dates from only 1920. The previous bandstand was of a conventional design, being a large circular affair with a conical roof. It was made rather unconventional by the addition of wheels, and a team of horses would drag the whole edifice to various points along the prom for the next performance.

5. Walk on, past the bandstand (J), and stop opposite St George's Hotel (K).

K. St George's is one of the grand old hotels of Llandudno. It was built for Isaiah Davies, who epitomised the thrusting young Victorian businessman superbly portrayed by Arnold Bennett in his novel, *The Card*, which is partly set in Llandudno. Like the book's hero, Denry Machin, Isaiah Davies was determined to grab every business opportunity that was offered by a rapidly expanding Victorian bathing resort. Isaiah was born in 1831 on a farm on the Great Orme, but at nineteen he shrewdly married the considerably older daughter of the licensee of the King's Head Inn. He soon inherited the inn and was delighted to entertain there the land agent of Lord Mostyn, Llandudno's major land owner. The story goes that the land agent, John Williams, ran up a huge drinking bill at the King's Head, and that Isaiah Davies generously offered to cancel the debt in exchange for the choice building plot on the new Llandudno promenade. So it came to pass and in 1855, at only 24 years of age, Isaiah Davies was the owner of Llandudno's first modern seafront hotel, the magnificent St George's.

6. Continue along the prom until you see the Punch and Judy tent (L),

L. *Codman's Punch and Judy* is a Llandudno tradition dating back to 1864 when Richard Codman arrived in his Gypsy caravan to perform his show. He claimed that he stayed beyond the holiday season because his horse dropped dead. It certainly wasn't because of the warmth of his welcome, because no sooner had he begun his performances than the Improvement Commissioners slapped a ban on him. Punch and Judy was considered too downmarket for Llandudno. Fortunately Codman appealed successfully and his family have been performing here ever since. Richard's son, John, was probably the best known showman as he expanded in the boom years of early cinema. He operated mobile fairground-style film shows all over Wales in the years just before the First World War. Like many of the other pioneers of the industry he didn't have sufficient capital to compete in the era of the Picture Palaces. After the war he promoted the occasional film and variety shows in Happy Valley until the mid-twenties, when the Council refused to renew his lease after a series of disputes.

and then continue onto the pier (M),

M. This is actually the second pier to be built on this site. The first was built in 1858 as part of an abortive scheme to develop Llandudno, or St George's as it would have been known, as a commercial port. The origins of that scheme go back to 1836 when Llandudno, along with Porth Dinllaen and Holyhead, was being proposed as one of the three candidates to be chosen by parliament as the major port for communications with Ireland. With the successful bridging of the Menai in 1850, Holyhead's supremacy was assured, but Llandudno's backers pushed ahead with a revised scheme. They published their detailed plans in 1853 but it took them five years to get the railway branch line into town, and to erect a basic pier structure. In the meantime they were being overtaken by events, and Llandudno was being developed in an altogether different direction. Fortunately for us the St George's Harbour pier was swept away by a storm in 1859, and its proposers gave up as they had failed to meet the time conditions laid out in the parliamentary act. Thus you see before you an elegant pleasure pier, and not an industrial harbour. The main pier was opened to the public in 1877, and the spur section on which you are standing was added in 1884. Unlike our Victorian promenaders, you may proceed without charge; it cost them four pence each to walk along the pier.

notice the ruins of the old Pier Pavilion (N) on your left, and the Grand Hotel (O) a little further along.

N. Since 1886, the Pavilion was the main venue on the pier for entertainments of all kinds. Its early fame arose as the concert home of the flamboyant Jules Rivière and his orchestra. In 1894, Rivière fell out with the Pier Company and set up his own concert hall further along the promenade, but by the turn of the century he had fallen out with the whole town and moved his company to Colwyn Bay. In later years other famous musicians who performed at the Pier Pavilion included Adelina Patti, Paul Robeson, The Beverly Sisters, Semprini and the Beatles, although sadly never on the same bill. Besides music, the Pavilion offered political speeches from Lloyd George, Oswald Mosely and Winston Churchill; comedy from George Formby, Robb Wilton and Arthur Haynes; as well as early cinema in the form of 'The American Bioscope'; and annual maypole dancing (if the weather precluded the use of Happy Valley). After years of disgraceful neglect, the Pavilion burnt down in 1994.

O. The Grand Hotel was opened in 1901, and embodied the success of Llandudno as a resort as it replaced two buildings originally designed to serve the new town but that were already proving too modest in the facilities they offered. The building that housed the baths, reading room and billiard hall had been opened in 1855, whilst its annexe, the Baths Hotel, had only opened in 1879 and was already being demolished. The new Grand was the last word in luxury with magnificent views, and for many years its one hundred and fifty-six bedrooms made it the largest hotel in Wales.

7. Proceed to the end of the pier (P).

P. Llandudno pier is an object of beauty. It offers a wonderfully bracing walk, but its most important function was to provide a landing place for steamers. Many holiday-makers arrived in Llandudno, particularly from Liverpool, by this route. On 20th July 1907, 3,181 passengers alighted at the pier end from the steamers of one company alone. For those who preferred to come to Llandudno by train, the steamers still offered a wonderful variety of day trips out to Anglesey, Southport, the Isle of Man, or many other destinations. The principal operator was the Liverpool & North Wales Steamship Company, and one of their most affectionately remembered paddle boats was La Marguerite. From her inaugural sailing in 1904 she regularly brought over a thousand trippers to Llandudno. Leaving Liverpool at 10.45am she arrived at the pierhead at 1.00pm, allowing day trippers four hours ashore before returning to Liverpool. In between times she offered a short return sail to the Menai Straits. The growth of motor transport inevitably led to the decline in the appeal of boat travel, and in 1969 the regular steamer services from Llandudno ended. Opportunities to sail from the pier are now rare, although there are occasional visits from the beautifully preserved paddle steamer The Balmoral Castle, and the ships of the Isle of Man Steamship Packet Company. At the turn of the century you could also have watched one of Professor Beaumont's spectacular diving shows. He used a megaphone to advise of the imminent performance of his 'Handcuff Dive'. With hands cuffed behind his back he would plunge into the sea, triumphantly appearing seconds later, to great applause, with handcuffs held aloft. For his nightly sensational 'Fire Dive', he was locked into a sack which was dowsed in flammable liquid and set alight. The resulting fireball made a spectacular flight into the sea and, well you can guess the rest . . . Happy days!

8. Return to the start of the pier but exit through the original entrance, turn right and continue to the castellated building (Q).

Q. This is one of the toll houses built when the roadway around the

Great Orme was constructed from an existing footway in 1878. The original path was constructed by a Reginald Cust between 1856 and 1858, and named after him. There was a one penny charge to walk the path which encircled the Orme but many walkers, including Prime Minister Gladstone, were not amused by its narrowness and sheer drops. In 1905 the toll for the four and a half mile Marine Drive was still only a penny for pedestrians, tuppence for cyclists, three pence for saddle horses, but for carriages it was six pence per horse.

9. Turn left and walk into Happy Valley (R).

R. The Victorian period guidebooks described Happy Valley as a 'veritable amphitheatre of loveliness . . . in the season a part of it is appropriated by a first class troupe of minstrels'. In the early days, performers operated from canvas tents but around the turn of the century a small, very pretty open theatre was built with the paying audience in front seated in deck chairs, whilst those standing on the slopes could add their coins to the collecting boxes. When this wooden theatre was burnt down in 1933 it was replaced by a supposedly more permanent structure. Entertainment continued into the nineteen seventies with Waldini and His Band, Charles Wade's Concord Follies, and latterly Alex Munro, but when the theatre burnt down again, it wasn't replaced and a hundred years of entertainment in Happy Valley came to an end.

10. Walk through Happy Valley and climb the stairs to the upper level of the colonade (1932). Continue, enjoying the views over the pier and sea, towards the town centre; descend the stairs near some stone-built public toilets (S).

S. These are Llandudno's oldest public toilets, opened in 1893. The bricked-up opening in the rock between the toilets and the colonade was originally an adit of the Ty Gwyn mine, and was later used as a wine cellar by the Baths Hotel, which was demolished and replaced by the present Grand Hotel or at least that's what it says in the guide books. In fact this site was opened-up by the Great Orme Exploration

Society in January 1991 who found the 'tunnel' only went back a few feet and could never have been an adit for Tŷ Gwyn. It was more likely a natural cavern or geological fault, bricked-up to secure the rock face.

11. Continue on around South Parade, and turn right onto Gloddaeth Street; continue past the roundabout and pause on the corner, outside the chemists (T), before walking along Gloddaeth Street to the Clarence Hotel (U).

T. For more than one hundred years this was Hooson's, one of Llandudno's best known shops.

U. THE CLARENCE HOTEL

CLARENCE HOTEL

R.A.C.   **FULLY LICENSED**   A.A.
CENTRALLY SITUATED FACING SEA

Well appointed Hotel with an electric lift.   Comfortable Lounges. Easy access to beach, trains, shops, and entertainments.
Telephones   -   -   Reception 6485   Visitors 645211

Address: Gloddaeth Street (tel. 01492-860193)

Refreshments: Sandwiches, cakes, snacks or full meals.

Description: The Clarence was named after the Duke of Clarence who died in 1892, the year the Hotel opened, when it was described as follows: 'The general impression is exceedingly pleasing owing to the walnut woodwork and furniture . . . around the sides are inviting lounges and settees of crimson Utrecht velvet and there are marble-topped tables placed here and there. The silver is of excellent quality . . . the knives have solid ivory handles, specially made. The Drawing Room presents a magnificent spectacle and from the soft toning of colour the effect is very soothing and conductive (sic) to repose . . . An extremely convenient and unique apparatus in the bedrooms is that called Royle's Toilet Aquarius . . . '

Over Gentle Hills to Gloddaeth

Walk Number:	Two
Distance:	Three miles
Terrain:	Mainly rough, dry but uneven pasture, some up hill
Start:	Craig-y-don Recreation Ground, Queen's Road, Llandudno
Finish:	Circular
Transport:	Central

Introduction:

Llandudno has many attractive buildings but its charm ultimately derives from its setting. The town is surrounded by hills and sea. This walk leads us over some of those gentle hills to one of the ancient country seats of the Mostyn family. This is a modified version of one of the most popular rambles taken by Victorian holiday-makers. Before the domination of the motor vehicle, hiking for miles through picturesque scenery was considered an essential part of a traditional holiday. The Red Guide to Llandudno (1905), advised that . . . 'Of the many pleasant walks in the immediate neighbourhood of Llandudno, that which lies through the woods of Gloddaeth is one of the most delightful'. However, Baddeley and Ward's 1892 guide to North Wales cautioned that . . . 'The grounds in front (of the house) can only be visited by privilege, and perhaps the chief attraction of the place to the sojourner in shadeless Llandudno is its umbrageous surroundings.' What more can I say?

The Walk and Points of Interest:

1. From the gates of the recreation ground, cross and enter the park opposite. Continue through the park to the corner at the far right, next to the telephone box; exit and continue along Roumania Drive, taking the second right, Princes Drive. Continue up to Tan-y-Bryn Road, cross and turn left, notice the big house on the right (A).

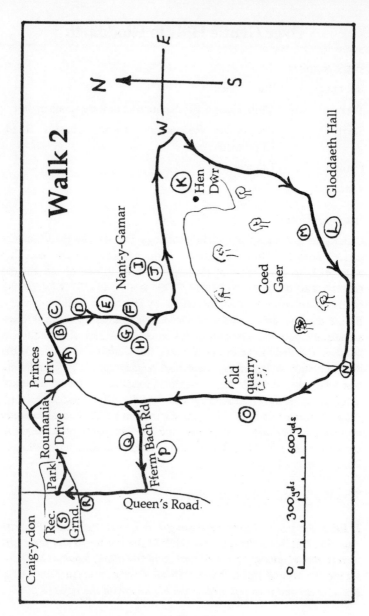

Walk 2

A. Tan-y-Bryn opened as a school in 1893. It was initially run by Charlton Felix Visinier Hall to 'prepare boys for Public Schools and the Navy'. Charlton Hall was an interesting character who was active in exploring and mapping the legendary lost lands of Llys Helig. He died on 17th March 1901 but the school continued, as the memorial on the gatepost records.

Continue to the houses on the corner (B).

B. This block of buildings was originally erected near the end of the nineteenth century by Charlton Hall of Tan-y-Bryn. It provided him with a stable and coach house, and a dwelling for the groom. Over the years the original buildings have been converted to provide three houses, Trevena, Rose Cottage and Quinta.

Notice on the other side of the road, amongst the trees, are the remains of small-scale quarrying (C).

C. This quarry, and the one further up behind Nantygamar Cottage, were developed around the middle of the nineteenth century to provide building stone for the rapidly growing town of Llandudno. Work continued for about a hundred years, with up to twenty people employed on site at times. Quarrying finally ceased in 1953.

2. Continue by walking up Nantygamar Road, noting en-route, Tegfryn (D) and the single storey part of Nantygamar Cottage (E).

D. Tegfryn began life as an army hut in Kinmel Camp near Prestatyn. It was erected here about 1920, and it was already a fortunate survivor for many other huts were smashed and set on fire when Canadian troops at the camp mutinied and rioted in March 1919. Red Flags were raised and five soldiers killed.

E. The single storey part of Nantygamar Cottage dates from the middle of the nineteenth century, with the two-storey part now forming the front added about twenty years later. This addition was begun by the then occupant, Edward Edwards, who was employed at the clay mine situated on the hill above the house. This clay was extracted from about 1850 to 1880, and was exported from the shore in flat-bottomed boats and eventually used in various potteries. The next occupant, Edward Owens, planned to collect water for the house in large stone tanks situated higher up, near the road. Before the system was even connected up, his small son had fallen into one of the tanks and drowned. The same fate then befell a horse, and so Edward sensibly decided to abandon the scheme and smashed the tanks; but you can still see their remain further on, below the road where it turns sharply to the left.

3. *Continue on up the road, on your left you can see the impressive remains of two limekilns (F). Also nearby are Hafod-y-bryn (G), and Nantygamar Farm (H).*

F. These two limekilns date from the early eighteenth century. The aim was to produce lime which could ultimately be used either as a mortar in building work or to spread on agricultural land to improve the fertility of the soil. The method used was to tip coal into the kiln from the top, then to add layers of crushed limestone. The coal was ignited through the fireplace at the front of kiln and then allowed to burn for about four days. The temperature would eventually rise to about 1000 degrees Celsius, driving off carbon dioxide from the limestone and leaving behind quicklime which could be raked out through the fireplace once the fire was exhausted. The limeburner had a wretched existence spending much of his time sheltering under a rude lean-to, and constantly tending the fires to ensure that a high temperature was maintained. The fumes were dreadful and the quicklime was highly caustic. The kilns seem to have fallen into disuse sometime around 1870. By then a variety of fertilizers, including nitrates from South America, were available to farmers, and commercial cement was widely available to builders.

G. Hafod-y-bryn was probably built by squatters on what was common land in the eighteenth century. It was acquired by the Mostyns after the enclosures, when it was occupied by David and Grace Hughes and their family. David was a copper miner, probably working on the Great Orme (Gogarth). The house was bought by Charlton Hall of Tan-y-bryn in 1873, who used it for staff accommodation in connection with his school. The school caretaker, George Hughes, eventually bought the freehold in 1918 having already occupied Hafod-y-bryn for several years.

H. Nantygamar Farm dates from 1870 and is interesting because of its connections with the quarries nearby. In fact it was originally called Quarry Cottage and early residents, the Hughes family, worked the Nantygamar quarries for many years.

4. Go through the metal kissing gate by the cattle grid. Ignore the deliberately off-putting private land signs because you do have the right to walk here, and follow the direction indicated by the yellow arrow sign. After about one hundred yards look back for you now get a better view of the two farmhouses which are now on your left; one looks old (J), and the other new (I).

I. If you look at the new farm, Castell y Gwylfryn, you can see that the outbuildings are old. In fact, this is the older farmstead. A fortified watching place or castle may well have stood on this prominent site, overlooking the approach of the Romans. The existing barns probably date from the early eighteenth century, and the house from the early 1980's.

J. The chimneys of Penymynydd immediately suggest an eighteenth century origin, and records bear this out. The single storey section of Penymynydd is said to have been a *Ty Unnos* thrown up on common land with smoke coming out of the chimney before dawn and so traditionally entitling the occupants to claim freehold rights. The enclosure act didn't recognise such traditional rights and, inevitably, it came under the control of the Mostyns. In the 1841 census the head of the household, Henry Edwards, gave his employment as a copper miner, probably on the Orme.

5. Continue walking until you reach the tower-type building (K).

K. This is Hen Dŵr, built as a windmill for Sir Roger Mostyn of Gloddaeth sometime in the first half of the seventeenth century. It probably lost its sails towards the end of the following century and may have ceased production even before that, but continued to be used as a dwelling. There was an old millhouse attached to the tower but this was demolished when the tower was renovated.

Continue walking, and stop when you meet a junction with another footpath. Take the path to your left, and continue for about four hundred yards until you reach the edge of a wood. Take a sharp right and continue down, following the path along the edge of this wood, entering the trees for a short while but quickly emerging again as a group of large old buildings appears before you; this is Gloddaeth Hall (L).

GLODDAETH.

L. Gloddaeth was for five hundred years the main local seat of the Mostyns. It was originally acquired through marriage in 1460. The oldest part of the present building is the Great Hall, said to date from 1584, with the majority of the rest being from the seventeenth century. Gloddaeth has a fascinating history. In 1582 it was the scene of the arrest of a Catholic priest, Father John Bennett who was condemned to death (but later reprieved). In 1650 Archbishop John Williams, celebrated prelate, reviled politician, and sometime owner of Marl Hall, died here. Llandudno's favourite, the Queen of Romania was entertained here in 1896 and in 1912 Lady Henrietta Augusta Mostyn passed away here. Gloddaeth is now the home of St David's School and the house and grounds are not open to the general public, although this was not always so. In the 1905 Red Guide to Llandudno, readers were informed that Gloddaeth Hall 'is open to the public on Tuesdays and Fridays, from 2 to 4 on the presentation of one shilling tickets, which can be procured from Llandudno tradesmen'.

6. Walk along the path which runs along the back of the Hall passing an old tower (M) on your right.

M. This building served as a water tower to Gloddaeth, holding spring water and providing a head of pressure before the Hall was connected to the Llandudno water mains in the 1880's.

Continue past the hall, after about 50 yards fork to your right, entering the trees. Ignoring the first comparatively modern building, you soon notice a lone black and white cottage behind an old limestone wall (N).

N. Sometimes referred to as Tudor Cottage this building is in fact Victorian, and was used as the laundry to serve the needs of the big house.

7. Pass behind the laundry house; go through a kissing gate, descend alongside a wall on your left, and notice the view over Llandudno. Continue to the next kissing gate, but do not go through it. Take the path which turns right, continue alongside the hedge and slightly above fields on your left, and soon you arrive at the rear of an old farm (O).

O. This is Fferm, which retains many features which betray its seventeenth century origins. There is a disused quarry on your right, behind the farm. Notice the massive remains of an old lime kiln. If you climb up to it, you can still make out the circle of stonework that looks a bit like a well. It was actually the portal for loading in the limestone, which was roasted over the fierce heat. Pack animals were used, as access was difficult and when one unfortunate creature fell down into the workings and was only extricated with great difficulty, the incident became immortalised in the local name for the quarry, the Donkey Pit.

8. Continue, cross the wall stile and continue to the end of the lane, turning left along Fferm Bach Road, next to a large institution (P).

P. This was opened in 1904 as The Lady Forester Convalescent Home. The Forester family owned quarrying and iron-making works in Shropshire and Llandudno was chosen as a healthy place for their workers to recuperate. Lady Forester was born plain Mary Anne Ricketts, in Meaford, Staffordshire, but she was no commoner. her father was a viscount and her first husband, Colonel David Ochterlonay Dyce Sombre was enormously wealthy and left her his entire fortune in his will. In 1862 she married Baron George Cecil Forester, an army general, Comptroller of the Royal Household, one time M.P. and Father of the House of Commons. When he died in 1886 she decided her own estate might be able to spare the odd three quarters of a million pounds to endow charitable works. On her death in 1893 the Charity was duly created and plans for two hospitals in Shropshire and this convalescent home in Llandudno were set in motion. The exterior of the building is dressed with red St Bees sandstone and the architect was Edward L'Anson. The central section was for staff accommodation with female convalescents in the North wing and males in the South and all surrounded by 18 acres of magnificent grounds. The main entrance lodges are in Queen's Road with the buildings we have just passed at the rear being the original stables and laundry. No longer the preserve of Shropshire workers the whole enterprise is now run as a private medical centre.

Notice a black and white house in its own grounds, across the road (Q).

Q. For more than sixty years this was Llandudno's local museum. It was initiated by Francis Chardon who had built up an eclectic collection in what was his private home. Chardon was rather fixated on his mother, and named his home Rapallo House after her. She was a daughter of Signor A.M. Rapallo who was alleged to have used his wealth to help Louis Napoleon become Emperor of France in 1852. When Chardon died in 1925 he bequeathed the house and its contents to the town. In recent years the museum has moved to Gloddaeth Street and the house is once again a private home.

9. Continue along Fferm Bach Road until you meet the junction with Queen's Road. Cross over, turn right, and continue until you reach the junction with Balfour Road. Notice the metal pole (R) protruding from the pavement near the corner.

R. This is the remaining bottom half of a water outlet provided to sluice horse droppings off the road, no laughing matter in 1900.

10. Continue along Queen's Road until you reach the entrance to the bowling green, refreshment is at hand. (S)

S. BOWLING GREEN CAFE

Address: Queen's Road Recreation Ground, Craig y Don

Refreshments: Tea, coffee, sandwiches, pies, crisps, cakes, etc.

Description: An old-fashioned park pavilion with a covered verandah for eating outside overlooking the tennis courts. A quaint, modest establishment in an attractive, convenient setting.

A Visit to the Holy City

Walk Number:	Three
Distance:	Two and a half miles
Terrain:	Moderate, some uphill, some may be muddy
Start:	Penrhynside bus stop, foot of Pendre Road
Finish:	Circular
Transport:	Buses 13, 14, 15, 16, approx. four per hour

Introduction:

One hundred years ago the chapel was the heart and soul of the Welsh village. The chapel offered education and social life as well as spiritual guidance. Where the established church was hierarchical, middle class and above all English, the chapels were controlled and created by local, usually Welsh, and working class, people. This walk explores a village that was so enthusiastic about chapel life that it built and ran four chapels, and then added a church for good measure; 920 holy seats for only 300 village bottoms. This is Penrhynside, a village that developed to house and serve the quarrymen of the Little Orme. A village that was better known to the old tram conductors as *The Holy City*.

The Walk and Points of Interest:

1. Walk up the hill until you notice a modern bungalow, on the right (A).

A. The bungalow name-plate, Sannan Lodge, provides a clue, for this was previously the site of the Church of St Sannan. Erected in 1925, the church was constructed of wood and corrugated metal. Originally it served not only Penrhynside, but also the communities of Bodafon and Pantywennol. In the early years there was a permanent lay leader, a thriving Sunday School, a highly regarded choir and a ladies' sewing guild. A wonderful pipe organ was donated in 1927 and for forty-three

Walk 3

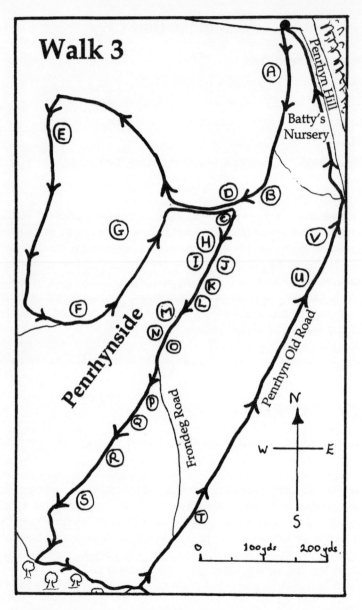

Penrhyn Hill

Batty's Nursery

Ⓐ

Ⓔ

Ⓓ Ⓑ

Ⓒ

Ⓖ

Ⓗ

Ⓘ Ⓙ

Ⓥ

Ⓚ

Ⓛ

Ⓤ

Ⓕ

Ⓜ

Ⓝ

Ⓞ

Penrhynside

Ⓟ

Ⓟ

Frondeg Road

Penrhyn Old Road

Ⓡ

Ⓢ

N

W — E

S

Ⓣ

0   100 yds   200 yds.

years the church had the same organist, Mrs Williams. Every Sunday there were three services each packed to capacity, but after the war attendance began to decline. The three services were reduced to one and the pipe organ was removed and sold. By 1978 the Sunday attendance had fallen to about a dozen worshippers. The church was closed, and services transferred to the village Mission Hall. Demolition followed, but if you look carefully alongside the road you might notice the old iron church gate, left as a poignant reminder.

2. Continue on up the hill until you notice the road branch steeply to the right, on your left is a terrace called Neville Place (B).

B. Number 1 Neville Place was the old Mission House before St Sannan's church was built, with the lay leader, Watkyn Powell, in residence. You might notice the old stained glass still intact in the rear windows (but remember that this is now a private house). Whist drives were held here every Thursday, organised by the Reverend ('Hearts are Trumps') Roberts. Declining attendances finally forced the closure of the Mission Rooms in 1997.

Look across to the village hall (C).

C. This was opened in 1892 as the Ebeneser Congregational Chapel. In those days knowledge of the bible was so widespread that reference to an episode of a bible story was as common a part of everyday speech as a modern reference to a TV soap episode. Everyone understood that the congregation here chose the name Ebeneser to characterise themselves as holy people, struggling against a hostile and Godless world as in the first book of Samuel, chapter 7, verses 5 to 14. The hostile and Godless world finally triumphed in the nineteen seventies; the chapel closed and the organ was transferred to Calfaria Chapel.

3. Ascend the hill, Bryn Gwynt Lane, but pause outside the corner house (D), on your right.

D. Originally this was Robert Owen's Penrhyn Stores which was a general grocery. By the nineteen twenties it had become a branch of the Colwyn Bay and District's Co-operative Stores, which it remained for the next fifty years.

4. Continue up the hill, bearing to the right, and continue until you notice a terrace of thirteen houses to your left (E).

E. This is officially called *Mount Pleasant Terrace* but it is better known as *Spion Kop,* in reference to its elevated situation, and its erection at the time of the eponymous South African battle. This terrace exemplifies the expansion of the village at the turn of the century, to cater for the influx of quarry workers employed on the Little Orme.

5. Continue past the old cast iron lamp post (on your right), and turn left along the lane at the back of the terrace. Notice the lovely old railings embedded in the undergrowth on your right, and then continue on through a field gate (wonderful views out over the bay). After about 50 yards, turn left off the lane and descend through a rocky field, emerging onto a lane. Turn left and continue downhill until you soon reach some houses. Notice a single storey cottage on your left (F).

F. This is Graig Lwyd Bach which retains some of the character of its eighteenth century origins, when Penrhynside was just a tiny settlement of scattered cottages, with its economy based mainly on agriculture.

6. Continue to follow the lane as it turns along to the left. After 100 yards or so you will see on your left, a black and white house with a long front garden. It has its name, Tan-y-Wal (G), on the gate.

G. Tan-y-Wal is another cottage with eighteenth century origins. At one time this was home to Huw Hughes, the village cobbler. He was notorious for his habit of chewing tobacco, and waiting customers had to be alert so as to avoid the soggy projectiles of ejected tobacco.

7. Descend and walk a little past the old Congregational Chapel until you notice a house, Beech House (H), turned at right angles to the road, on your right.

H. This is Beech House, and the window up against the street had an awning and was the shop window of Alfred Cook's greengrocery. This shop continued as a greengrocers, with various alterations and proprietors, for about seventy years.

8. Continue along Pendre Road to the Penrhyn Arms (I).

I. When an enterprising Englishman took over the licence of the Penrhyn Arms in the early years of the century, Ochor Pen was a totally Welsh speaking village. He immediately found that the regulars deserted him *en masse* and transferred their custom to Thomas Williams at the Cross Keys. His business was a spectacular failure.

Opposite the pub is Mona House (J), and a little further along are the Post Office (K), and Calfaria Chapel (L).

J. Mona House, after the war, was Hampson's Dairy. Mrs Hampson ran the shop whilst her husband, Albert, went round the houses on his motorbike, ladling the required amount of milk into customers' jugs from the churn nestling in the sidecar. Although an Englishman, Mr Hampson was polite enough to greet his customers with a friendly, 'Sut mae pobl yn y ty heddiw?'

K. The present Post Office was previously the Penrhyn Stores, run by Henry Owen and selling general groceries.

L. Calfaria Baptist Chapel was built in 1894. There had been Baptists living in Penrhynside since 1815, but previously they had walked to the chapel in Glanwydden. When the quarries were booming and two

Gwefus gwirionedd A SAIF BYTH; OND TAFOD CELWYDDOG NI SAIF FUNUD AWR. DIARHEBION, XII, 19.

hundred people had already filled the pews to capacity, worshippers often had to bring their own chairs from home to avoid standing. When Robert Owen of Tan-y-graig (next to the Village Hall) was precentor, the chapel had a renowned reputation for its choirs. Calfaria's Gymanfa Ganu was quite famous, but sadly by the nineteen seventies all was in decline.

9. More or less opposite Calfaria Chapel is a design-company building (M).

M. This building was the Penrhynside Sub-Post Office with Edward Williams as the Postmaster. The section on the right was run as the Post Office Stores, which was a grocers and drapers shop. By the nineteen twenties it had become a hardware store, with a fish and chip shop next door. The chip shop continued for another fifty years.

The next house on the right is Bryn Masarn (N), and

N. Bryn Masarn was the home of Madame Rose who was a palmist. This was a risky business at the turn of the twentieth century, with the local Constabulary out to get them. In July 1911, a Madame Jeanette was caught in Llandudno, prosecuted, and fined one pound with costs.

opposite is the Moriah Wesleyan Chapel (O).

O. Mount Moriah in Jerusalem was where Solomon built his temple after the Lord had appeared there to David, his father (2nd Chronicles, chap. 3, vs 1). This Moriah however was opened in 1887, and although the land was donated, the building cost £440. Quarry workers got paid about one pound a week, and chapel buildings required a huge financial commitment from their congregations. Nevertheless at Moriah, they were soon expanding the chapel to include a schoolroom and kitchen. In more recent years there was a new pipe organ installed, a public address system, gas central heating and general refurbishment and it seemed, for a while, that Moriah might be able to halt the decline afflicting the other chapels. By the seventies membership stood at about fifty, and funds were augmented from time to time by organising special train shopping trips to places like Leeds and Coventry. They maintained their fortnightly Literary Society and their weekly Sunday School. There was an active Women's Sewing Class, and even two services every Sunday. But in recent years the decline has set in here too . . .

10. Continue, and cross the end of the road that descends to the left. Notice the houses on the corner, on your left, (P).

P. The first house on the corner, number one Ty Llwyd Villas, was originally James Jones' Pioneer Stores, which began as a general grocers but later acquired a reputation for the excellence of its cakes. The shop is no longer, but locals still refer to the descent as 'Siop Cakes Hill'.

11. Continuing ahead, noticing the fourth house on your left (Q), and further ahead on your left again, Saron Chapel (R).

Q. The fourth house on the left is Rock Villa, for many years the home of a joiner called Richard Williams. He was known to all as Dick Rock Villa, the much loved father of the Penrhynside Brass Band.

R. The Saron Calvinistic Methodist Chapel opened in 1897, and is named in reference to the mutual love of Christ and his church (Song of Solomon, chap.2, vs 1). Previously the congregation held meetings in the stables down at Penrhyn Old Hall. David Evans of Pen-y-cae (which we will pass in a few minutes) was an enthusiastic leader of this early band of believers. He was one of the deacons who arranged to pay £144 for a freehold site, and £628 for the chapel building. The large site gave them room to also erect five houses, which you can still see today; two adjacent to, and three below, the chapel. Selling off these houses has enabled Saron to get an injection of cash in times of financial crisis. The chapel has a fine American organ which was given in memory of three young lads who were killed in the Great War. The singing at Saron was highly regarded, and also much appreciated was the music of Mrs Agnes Roberts who played the organ for more than fifty years. Sadly, Saron has also declined in recent years.

12. Continue to the end of the second terrace of houses (S).

S. The final house, 1 Woodbine Terrace, was the home of the Congregational Minister of Ebeneser Chapel (C), the Reverend William Phillips. The power of the Almighty may also have interested the Williams family at number 6 when their house was struck by lightning in July 1932. Despite breaking a window, scorching the curtains, burning the wiring and smashing the wireless the family escaped uninjured.

13. Go through the gate and pass through in front of Pen-y-cae. At the end of the path, turn left and continue down through the trees. After about one hundred yards, you cross the stile and turn left along the road. Continue along the old, unpaved roadway and after about one hundred yards, notice a metal sign attached to the wall on the right (T).

T. This is the legacy of a fascinating dispute that occurred about eighty years ago. Barratt Carrington Sellars J.P. bought Penrhyn Old Hall and decided that he would no longer allow the public to pass along the lane here. The Council reminded him that this was a public highway and they instructed workmen to remove the physical barriers that he repeatedly placed across the lane. At one point Mr Carrington Sellars J.P. actually grabbed the Highway Authority's Surveyor by the throat and punched him in the face. It took several years to satisfactorily re-establish public access, and this sign indicates the grudging acceptance of your right to pass.

14. Continuing along Penrhyn Old Road and we soon come to our refreshment stop, the old home of Mr Carrington Sellars (U).

U. PENRHYN OLD HALL

Address: Penrhyn Old Road, Penrhyn Bay (tel. 01492-549888)

Refreshments: Excellent value bar meals, plus restaurant service.

Description: Largely sixteenth century with many characterful features to be seen inside. The Old Hall Estate originally comprised of several hundred acres, and stretched across most of Penrhyn Bay. During the Victorian period the land was gradually sold off, and early in the new century it operated mainly as a very successful museum of Welsh Antiquities. This ended when the proprietor went down with the Lusitania. Then began the reign of Carrington Sellars. In recent years various enterprises have been tried, and the present quirky bar and restaurant are much recommended.

15. Exit, turn left and continue until you notice a tall, ruined barn-type building (V) at the far side of a field, on your left.

V. This sad ruin is the early sixteenth century private chapel of the Pughs of Penrhyn Old Hall. It was repaired and in regular use as a church as recently as 1929. Its present state is a disgrace.

Continue, turning left on the corner, and bear left again along the green road, past the lodge. Return to our original starting place.

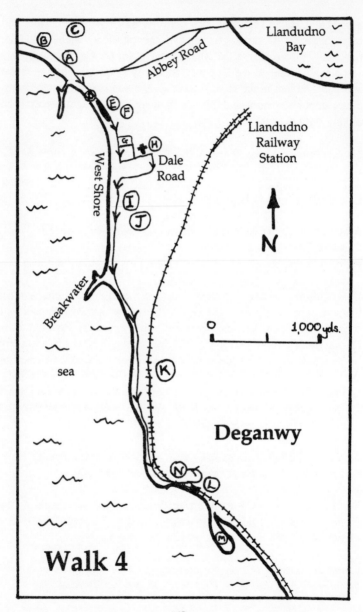

Llandudno
Bay

Abbey Road

West Shore

Llandudno
Railway
Station

Dale
Road

N

Breakwater

sea

1,000 yds.

Deganwy

Walk 4

From Dodgson to Deganwy

Walk Number: Four

Distance: Three miles

Terrain: Very easy, level, mostly across sand dunes and beaches

Start: Gogarth Abbey Hotel, West Shore, Llandudno

Finish: Castle Hotel, Deganwy

Transport: Central start. Return by train from Deganwy Station, (approx. 6 per day); or buses 12, 14, 15 or 16 (approx. 4 buses per hour).

Introduction:

> Lewis Carroll, as you know, was a frequent visitor to Llandudno as a guest of Dean Liddell at Gogarth Abbey, and it was Lewis Carroll's rambles on the West Shore with Dean Lidell's little girl, Alice, that inspired him to write the book and it is known that Lewis Carroll would read his manuscript to Dean Lidell's family at the fireside in the evening at Gogarth Abbey.

So claimed a booklet published by the Llandudno Memorial Committee in 1933. On this walk we will examine some of the places, and some of the claims, associated with the Alice in Wonderland story. We then continue across the dunes to Deganwy Docks.

The Walk and Points of Interest:

A. The Gogarth Abbey Hotel, famous as the home of Alice in Wonderland was built in 1862 as Penmorfa, a private house, for the Very Reverend Henry Liddell, Dean of Christchurch College, Oxford. It was his daughter, Alice, who provided the inspiration for Lewis Carroll's well known book (published 1865). Carroll, or rather Charles Lutwidge Dodgson, was a friend of Dean Liddell, and is said to have shared numerous holidays with him here. It is here that he is thought to have tried out the twists and turns of his Wonderland story on the family, reading to them from his manuscript which had been inspired by his day's activities with young Alice. The Reverend Liddell is thought to have been portrayed as the rather dreamy *Red King*, whilst Mrs Liddell, who Carroll is known to have fallen out with, is thought to be the tyrannical, socially ambitious, *Queen of Hearts,* with her croquet parties and summary executions. Dean Liddell sold the house to a colleague from Oxford in 1871. Since then the house has been added to and altered, but the original four storey section with the dormer windows can still be clearly recognised.

1. From the Gogarth Abbey Hotel (A), look to the left along the Marine Drive, and notice the small crenellated building (B) near the shore.

B. This is one of the two toll-houses, built to serve the new Marine Drive which was opened in 1878. This one seems to have been built as the more modest, junior partner to its North Shore companion (Walk One).

Look up at the cliffs of the Orme, behind the tollhouse, and notice the mouth of a cave (C) in the cliff face.

C. This is Ogof Arth, which has proved a desirable residence over the years. Besides the bear (Arth) it was notably the home of John Stephens and more recently Gwilym Hughes. John Stephens claimed to have lived there for at least fourteen years, and was fortunate enough to have been given an iron bedstead by Lady Augusta Mostyn when she paid him a social call in the 1850's. Gwilym Hughes was so comfy that he eventually had to be evicted by Llandudno Council, who gave him a council flat. Some have suggested that the cave entrance might have given Carroll the plot idea of 'falling down the hole into Wonderland'!

2. Walk a little along the prom, until you come to a statue of a rabbit

(D). To your left you will see a boating pond (E), and a circular tram shelter (F).

D. The inscription reads, 'On this very shore during happy rambles with little Alice Liddell, Lewis Carroll was inspired to write that Literary Treasure *Alice in Wonderland,* which has charmed children for generations.' This is the legacy of the 1933 Llandudno Lewis Carroll Memorial Committee quoted in the introduction to this walk. It was unveiled on 6th September 1933 by David Lloyd George, M.P. In his dedication speech he said; 'The man we are commemorating was one of the really great men of the world. It was a holiday at Llandudno that did this. He breathed our invigorating air, he had the sea that stimulates thought, the mountains to elevate him, and a child to lead him.'

E. The boating pond was opened in 1896 and receives water from the adit which drains the old Orme mine workings. Now used mainly for paddling, it was really designed for model yachts. In the old days, races were organised and were so popular that the council discussed how they could ensure that children were not consistently crowded out by adult participants.

F. The elegant circular tram shelter was originally provided for passengers of the Llandudno and Colwyn Bay Electric Railway Company. The line actually extended along West Parade to Dale Street, and was originally authorised to continue to Deganwy, but from its inauguration in 1907 passenger receipts for this section from Llandudno central were very disappointing. Consequently many trams were turned around before they even reached West Shore. The onward march of progress swept away the last tram on 24th March 1956.

3. Continue along West Parade until you spot a bungalow on the corner of Lloyd Street West, with a distinctive silvered onion-dome (G).

G. This is Castleside Bungalow, now Sheraton, which was the 1914 home of May Jones. Nowadays, bungalows are sought by the settled and the sober, but in 1914 they were still considered rather bohemian, which is a reflection of their exotic colonial origins. This was just the thing for May Jones who was not easily bound by pre-war conventions. A keen supporter of female suffrage; a passionate sportswoman; and a pioneer of transport, she had previously become the first woman to drive a motor car in Birmingham. In June 1914 she became the first Llandudno woman to fly. The pilot, Fred Raynham, picked her up from the beach and flew around over the town, finishing with a spectacular spiral dive and landing his seaplane safely in Llandudno Bay. Stepping out onto the beach May Jones pronounced her flight to have been simply, 'ripping'.

4. Turn up Dale Road and cross to the church (H).

H. The Church of Our Saviour is rather Arts & Crafts in design but its main interest for us lies inside, and it's only open for Sunday services (currently at 10am, not first Sunday in the month, and at 5pm on the 2nd and 4th Sundays). The church was consecrated on 30th July 1912 when the font was also specially dedicated by Bishop Watkin Williams of Bangor, a former pupil of Charles Dodgson. The plaque reads; 'This tablet records the fact that the font in this church was the gift of children in memory of Lewis Carroll (C.L. Dodgson), the author of Alice in Wonderland, and a lover of Llandudno'.

5. Return to the shore and continue walking south over the dunes (I), passing the North Wales Golf Club (J).

I. This area was traditionally used as a Warren and is marked as such on old maps. It was a favourite walking place of Alice Liddell, and she mentioned it in her letter to the 1933 memorial committee: 'I still have the happiest memories of Penmorfa, as my father's house at Llandudno was then called, and of the rambles over the Great Orme's Head and among the Llandudno sand hills . . . and . . . the days spent with Mr Dodgson'. The rabbits would have been far more numerous then, and could have provided inspiration for the famous White Rabbit of the story. It all sounds idyllic and a wonderful theme for our walk, but modern research has shown that Llandudno's claims on Carroll's story are fantasy. It is extremely unlikely that he ever set foot in Llandudno. The idea for *Alice in Wonderland* almost certainly arose during a boating trip in Oxford on 4th July 1862, when Carroll was entertaining the three little Liddell girls. Alice's 1933 letter was at first taken as confirming the Llandudno link, but a more careful reading makes it clear that her days with Dodgson may not be connected with her Llandudno adventures at all. Most serious researchers feel that Llandudno's claims on Carroll owe more to wishful thinking, and a commercial desire to boost tourism, than to any real evidence. Yet the old claims are constantly repeated in the press and publicity. Recent criticism has focused on Dodgson's personality and motivation, and particularly his possibly unhealthy interest in little girls. It may be the Liddells' growing awareness of this aspect of his relationship with their daughters that caused his later estrangement from the family.

J. North Wales Golf Club began in 1893 with a nine-hole course, which was soon extended. In 1895 a young professional called Fred Collins was engaged, and he did much to establish the name of the club throughout the golfing world. Having made his first public appearance at the now largely forgotten Trefriw Golf Course, he was active in establishing the Professional Golfers Association in 1902. In 1903 and 1904 he played for England in four international matches, and in 1905 he won the Welsh Open.

6. At the far end of the golf course, notice some white painted modern houses (K) just across the railway line, just before a footbridge.

K. This housing estate replaced the fondly remembered Deganwy Lido. The Lido, also called The West Shore Bathing Pool, opened in August 1934. The open-air pool was two hundred and ten feet long and one hundred feet wide, with an adjoining diving pool with springboards and water chutes. There was a large restaurant which also served as a concert and dance hall. There were one thousand lockers for swimmers, and seating around the pool for about eight thousand spectators. Besides the obvious attractions of swimming and sun-bathing there were talent shows, beauty contests, synchronised swimming and firework displays. Guide books described it as 'A temple of health and pleasure'. Uncle Mac, Gilbert Harding, Sandy MacPherson and many others performed at the Lido. In 1954 the Radio Luxembourg programme 'People Are Funny', with contestants performing amusing stunts to win televisions or radios, was broadcast from here. But it proved increasingly difficult to attract holiday makers. A 'Zoo' was added to the attractions, but as it contained animals more modest in both character and number than the average pet shop, this did little to halt the slide. In the late 1950's the Lido was bought by a property developer and demolished.

7. Continuing along the shore and enjoy the views across the estuary. You soon reach Marine Crescent, which you follow over the level crossing to the railway station (L).

L. Deganwy Station opened in 1866 as the only intermediate station on the branch line to Llandudno. The original building was most attractive, but the railways allowed the station to fall into chronic disrepair. Just as it looked as if a brewery were prepared to renovate the building and reopen it as a hostelry, the rail company announced that the station was structurally dangerous and demolition promptly followed. The original signal box, with its slightly unusual stone plinth, has survived.

The old quay (M) can be seen from the footbridge, and although it provides an attractive and interesting walk for local people, there is no official right of way.

M. Built by the LNWR between 1873 and 1879, the quay is about two hundred and thirty yards by about ninety yards, and encloses a harbour of about the same dimensions. It was planned mainly as a trans-shipment depot for slates which came down from Blaenau Ffestiniog in one hundred and fifty narrow gauge quarry trucks, piggy-backed onto fifty specially adapted standard gauge waggons. The slates were lifted onto ships for onward travel by sea. Two dockside cranes remain intact, whilst the metal pivot post of the other remains *in situ* nearer the railway. The main bodies of the three capstans remain in their original positions, although they are a little damaged. There was also a short narrow gauge railway on the quay itself, but nothing of this remains. The quay was a financial disaster from the beginning. Between 1886 and 1914 only 1,507 vessels used the dock, an average of about one a week. By 1913 that meant only nine boats over the whole year. But the quay limped on, with the last commercial vessel leaving in 1932.

8. Notice and return to our refreshment stop (N), next to the station.

N. THE CASTLE HOTEL

Address: Beach Road, Deganwy (tel. 01492-583555)

Refreshments: Bar meals, snacks and full restaurant menu

Description: Originally built about 1850 as a farmhouse called Tregonwy House, the Castle Hotel has been a Deganwy landmark for many years. It is a bit neglected, but still full of character.

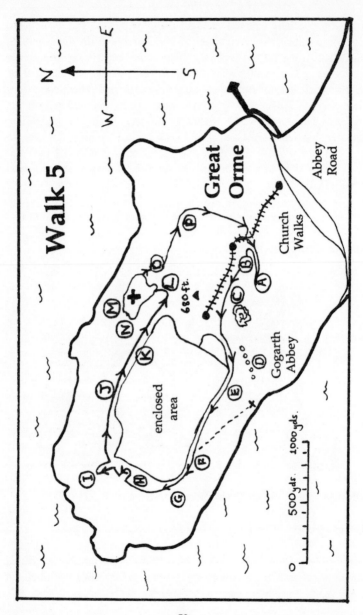

Walk 5

Great Orme

Abbey Road

Church Walks

Gogarth Abbey

enclosed area

680 ft.

500 yds. 1000 yds.

Ancient History on the Great Orme

Walk Number:	Five
Distance:	Four miles
Terrain:	Elevated but surprisingly level, well defined paths, dry surface in almost all weathers; but can be windy.
Start:	Halfway station on the Great Orme Tram
Finish:	Circular
Transport:	Great Orme Tramway is most convenient, with approximately four per hour April to October; bus number 73, every half hour

Introduction:

Llandudno began on the heights of the Great Orme. It is an ancient settlement. The English name is thought to derive from the Norse, when Viking marauders likened the appearance of the limestone headlands to a serpent. Their name stuck and has come down to us as Orme which shares the same derivation as 'The Worm's Head' in South Wales. The Welsh name for the area is Gogarth, and both the Norse 'Orme' and Welsh 'Gogarth' have existed together for many centuries. Yet the settlement on the Orme goes back much further than the Viking period. More than ten thousand years ago people were living in the caves dotted about the Orme. They used simple stone tools. By about 3,000 B.C. they were making pots and cultivating the land. By 1,500 B.C. they were digging out copper to combine with other minerals to produce a new wonder material; the Bronze Age had arrived in Llandudno. This walk illustrates these ancient times, and shows a little of subsequent developments.

The Walk and Points of Interest:

1. After leaving the tram, walk back a little down Tŷ-Gwyn Road, go through the gate next to the cattle grid and turn into St Beuno's Road on the right. After one hundred yards or so, turn into

Cromlech Road, and go over the stile to view the cromlech (A).

A. This Cromlech is called Llety'r Filiast (the Greyhound's Lair) whilst this part of the Orme is referred to as Maes y Facrell (the field of mackerel) possibly because it is a sheltered spot that was used for drying the catch in the sun to preserve it. About 5,000 years ago this cromlech was built as a burial chamber by Neolithic people. It would originally have been covered with a shell of soil and turf, and may have served a dual purpose of also staking the group's right to use the surrounding area of territory. It has sustained considerable damage over the years, but remains a powerful image of life and death in the New Stone Age.

2. Retrace your steps back up Cromlech and St Beuno's Roads until you reach the junction, on the left, with Pyllau Road. Just ahead of you, on the right, are the buildings of the Bronze Age Copper Mine Centre (B).

B. A tour of these workings is highly recommended, because unlike many 'visitor attractions' this provides an intelligent experience with a resident archaeologist who will answer your most searching queries. There is an admission charge (tel. 01492-870447) but you can visit the bookshop and café (our later refreshment stop) without charge.

This Bronze Age Copper Mine is a heritage site of world importance. The oldest workings contained stone hammers, bone tools and charcoal which was carbon dated to about 1,200 B.C. A complex network of galleries has been discovered over an area of six acres, and extending to a depth of over 250 feet. The Bronze Age miners used stone hammers to bash out the ore from the softer, easier to work rocks. The hammers themselves were selected from hard, rounded volcanic rocks they found on local beaches. When harder seams had to be penetrated, firesetting techniques were used. In easily worked areas simple tools of bone or antler were also used. Some of the galleries are very small, and suggest that children may well have helped mine for copper. These mines may have been abandoned when iron took over from bronze as the cutting edge material. It seems they may have been left unworked until they were reopened in the seventeenth century. In 1991 they were finally opened to the public.

3. Keep to the path on the left of the road, notice the quarried area (C) to your left.

C. The fossil quarry contains the remains of the oldest inhabitants of the Orme. Here are the shells of the creatures which lived in shallow seas 300 million years ago. The Bishop's quarry alludes to its ownership by the Bishop of Bangor, who was granted the manor of Gogarth by Edward I soon after his success in the war of 1277. As Lord of the Manor, Bishop Anian had a substantial palace built for himself below you, nearer the shoreline on a lower level of the Orme. (It is now in ruins, and on the private land of the Old Abbey Residential Home.)

4. When you see an area ahead that has been fenced off to protect the heathland, turn left along the edge of the fence and continue until you notice a series of shallow pits (D) on your left.

D. These pits held vertical *Brammock rods*. These were hinged so as to transmit movement horizontally, from a water powered engine below you on the shoreline, to a mine pump situated 1300 yards further up the slope. This arrangement didn't prove very effective and was replaced by a more efficient steam engine powered pumping system.

5. Following the path round to the right, notice a dried-up spring (E).

E. Ffynnon Gogarth provided the water to power the 'Tom and Jerry' (named after characters in a book published in 1821) engine, which operated the Brammock rods.

Continuing ahead, notice a descending path (F) on your left (the Monks' Path).

F. The 'Monks' Path' connected the Bishop's palace with St Tudno's church on the other side of the Orme. As Lord of the Manor of Gogarth his tenants would have had to fulfil certain duties, such as labour service and grinding corn at the Lord's mill, as well as paying an annual cash rent. There is therefore no doubt that this has long been an important path. Traditionally it was known as Ffordd Las, and the 'Monks' Path' name seems to have been a Victorian romanticization, loosely based on fact, but mainly devised to promote the areas charms for tourist purposes. The story goes that the path will miraculously remain green throughout the course of the longest drought because it was blessed by the passage of so many Holy Monks through the ages.

6. Do not descend the Monks' Path, but continue to follow your original route which continues around the outside of the old stone wall. The views are wonderful and this section is particularly peaceful. Soon, you reach a pile of stones (G) to your left.

G. This is thought to be a Bronze Age cairn or communal burial place, although passing walkers have undoubtedly added to the pile of stones.

7. Continue around the headland but stay at the same elevation. Before you turn to the east, notice a pit (H) about eighty yards from the wall.

H. This sink hole is an entirely natural phenomenon caused by the action of water on soluble limestone. The surrounding area is a limestone pavement with characteristic 'cracks' or grykes, which provide a sheltering environment for small plants.

Notice a standing stone (I) about two hundred yards to the north.

I. The exact role of this standing stone has not been clearly identified though, over the years, many have argued for an astronomical or mystical significance.

8. Follow the path until you notice a huge, distinctly unusual rock (J) off to the left.

J. The distinctive shape of this rock has been likened to that of the traditional 'cottage loaf'. When life in Llandudno was centred on the Orme, it was common practice for deals to be sealed by striking this rock. This explains its local name of, 'The Free Trade Loaf'. Like most of the huge, detached blocks of stone around you (and unlike the standing stone at [I]) this arrived here through nature, and not by design. It is an example of a glacial erratic, a boulder carried along like a pebble in a stream, by the huge and powerful glaciers of the Ice-Age. As the climate improved, the ice melted, and the boulders were left high and dry.

9. Continue, and soon you notice a water source (K) set into the wall on your right.

K. This is the Roman Well. Nearly two thousand years ago, the Romans forced their slaves to dig the ore from these mines and wash away the impurities here in these waters. Except that the stonework seems much more recent, and there is no evidence of Roman mining anywhere on the Great Orme! The masonry is most likely Victorian, and so is the story. The Victorians were adept at devising tall stories for gullible tourists like 'The Monks' Path' or Gelert's Faithful Hound, or the ludicrous re-naming of Llanfair Pwllgwyngyll.

10. If you look down on the slopes below you, and also to the area above the churchyard, you will notice ridges in the turf (L).

L. These ridges are the remains of medieval farming. The use of oxen and heavy wooden ploughs left behind characteristic furrows. As arable farming was increasingly confined to lower levels, these slopes were given over to grazing, and where they were not obliterated by subsequent mine works the evidence persists. The use of aerial photography has greatly facilitated the expert interpretation of such evidence in recent years.

11. Walk down to examine Saint Tudno's Church (M) and its burial grounds (N).

M. Tudno was a sixth century Celtic missionary and it is interesting to note that Celtic churches were often named after their founders, whereas those of the Roman Church were usually dedicated to well-known saints or martyrs. Tudno probably built himself a simple wattle and daub shelter (or possibly even made do with a cave), whilst he set about establishing a church here on the Orme. His original church building would probably have been of wood, cut down from the trees that were then much more numerous on the Orme. In the twelfth century a stone church was built, which was then enlarged in the fifteenth century. This building had its roof ripped off in a gale in 1839. The old church was abandoned and the new St George's Church, further down in the newly developing town, was consecrated in 1840 as the new parish church. Fortunately St Tudno's was re-roofed and restored in 1855, and in the summer, it still continues its long tradition of open air services.

N. In the new cemetery, surmounted by an astonishing (and easy to spot) white old-style winged motor racing wheel, is the grave of Beatrice Blore Browne, 1887-1921, with the brief epitaph, 'She Feared Naught But God'. Beatrice and her husband pioneered motoring in North Wales. In 1911 they organised a successful publicity stunt which involved driving four Darracq cars up to the summit of the Great Orme. Nearby lies the simpler headstone of a family; 'Who Lost Their Lives in the Dolgarrog Disaster of November 2nd 1925', when a dam burst and swept away much of the original Conwy Valley village. Up in the corner, away from the sea and slightly overgrown, is a splendid monument in relief of a Victorian hiker, with the epitaph: 'Erected with sincere affection and esteem to William Smith by the Llandudno mountaineering club and friends. In remembrance of many hours of good fellowship, 1899.'

Near to the church in the old graveyard there are five more gravestones of particular historical interest. Alice Tarrey lost her life on the wooden paddle steamer, the *Rothsay Castle,* which began to take in water off the Orme whilst on a voyage in bad weather from Liverpool to Menai. She sank on the 17th August 1831 drowning Alice and one hundred and eight other passengers. The son of John Bright, the well known Victorian statesman has a simple white headstone announcing that he died 'aged nearly six, November 8th, 1864'. Jonathan Rawlings died 1836; George Edwards died 1813; and William James died 1827; were all agents for copper mines on the Orme. Each has a horizontal slate headstone which provide further details of their lives.

12. Leave the churchyard by the gate to the south-east, cross the road, and follow the marked path until you soon notice a spring on your right (O).

O. Ffynnon Powell is named after the family that brought it into being! Distressed by the persistence of a summer drought they retired to St Tudno's to implore God's help. After a serious session of prayer they began to return home along this track when, lo and behold, they realised that God had indeed responded. Bubbling up from the ground was the never failing water supply you see before you.

Continue along the track until you reach an old farm (P).

P. This is Penymynydd Isaf which is also called the Pink Farm; away to the right you should also be able to see Penymynydd Ucha, which is sometimes called the White Farm. Both farmhouses are substantially eighteenth century dwellings, although farming has been carried on here for much longer. Both farms quickly realised that there was money to be made from the influx of Victorian ramblers on the Orme and both operated as refreshment rooms. This became 'The Farm Inn', which had a full drinks licence, but alas no more.

13. Follow the lane on the right, and soon you should be able to recognise the starting point of our walk, from the halfway station you can return to the town by tram; but it is recommended to first continue across to the Copper Mines complex (B) for refreshments and underground explorations . . .

B. COPPER MINES TEA ROOM

Address: Pyllau Road, Great Orme, Llandudno, tel. 01492-870447

Refreshments: Tea, coffee, soft drinks, sandwiches, cakes, baked potatoes and cooked meals

Description: Although part of the Great Orme Bronze Age Copper Mine complex the cafe building itself has no great history but it is attractively decorated, quiet and the food is good. You can eat here and visit the bookshop even if you choose not to take the tour of the mine workings.

The Countess and the Royal Mail

Walk Number: Six

Distance: Three miles

Terrain: A level, paved, town-trail type walk, apart from a couple of flights of stairs; ordinary shoes and clothes are suitable

Start: Llandudno Junction Railway Station

Finish: Circular

Transport: Train from Llandudno (five trains per day from Monday to Saturday); numerous buses at other times

Introduction:

This is not the most scenic walk in the book. Some parts are quite grim, and there are signs of neglect and dereliction all around. This is not the face of Llandudno presented to tourists, and yet it is a crucial part of the history of the area, Llandudno Junction exploded around the railway. This was the key depot on the North Wales Coast. Trains not only passed through *en-route* between Chester and Holyhead, but also between Llandudno and Blaenau Ffestiniog. The Junction naturally housed many people directly employed by the railways, and also the carters, coalmen and cabmen serving a secondary function. Then there were all the shops and services necessary to supply the first groups of workers, and then the banks to provide financial support to these shopkeepers. Within seventy years of the coming of the trains, the Junction had been transformed from a rural backwater with a few scattered dwellings to a busy, commercial, industrial, residential and transport centre. Seventy years further on the action had moved elsewhere; the Junction was in sad decline . . .

The Walk and Points of Interest:

A. The main line from Chester had reached this point by 1848, but there was no station here. Passengers for Llandudno had to alight at

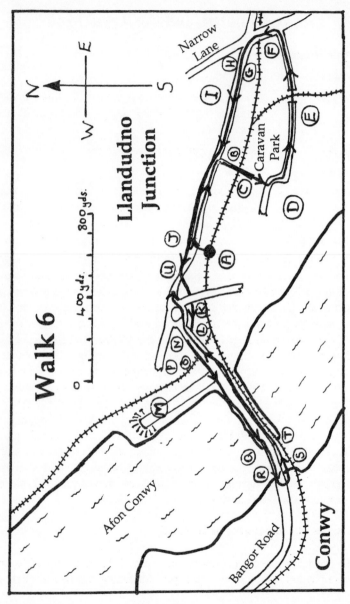

Walk 6

Llandudno Junction

Narrow Lane

Caravan Park

Afon Conwy

Bangor Road

Conwy

0 400 yds. 800 yds.

N
W   E
S

Colwyn or Conwy and travel onwards by horse-drawn coach. Isaiah Davies, proprietor of St George's Hotel, ran a regular coach service that connected Llandudno with trains from Conwy, from 1856. With the construction of the Llandudno branch line, Llandudno Junction came into being; but the station was built about a quarter of a mile to the west, in the fork of the main and branch lines. That site soon proved to be too congested, and in 1897 the present station was opened and the old one demolished. Much of the paraphernalia of the old steam train era has now been swept away but you might be able to spot the huge old carriage shed of 1899, to the south, if you move along the platform. This is the last remaining example of a L.N.W.R. shed in North Wales, and a testament to the importance of the Junction as a concentration depot for North Wales, with Bangor, Holyhead and Rhyl all being subsidiaries.

1. You start at Llandudno Junction Station (A), where there is much to see. When you cross the footbridge and make your way out of the station you will pass the original ticket office, just inside the main station entrance.

From the entrance, take the Conwy road to your right, and continue for about four hundred yards until you reach Queens Road on the right. Just before you cross the bridge, look down on the ground to your left (B).

B. Can you spot a rare survival; an old metal boundary marker of the London and North Western Railway? The original promoter, the Chester to Holyhead Railway Company was absorbed by the L.N.W.R. in 1867. That was bad news for Welsh-speaking railwaymen. When the District Engineer requested a Welsh translation of the L.N.W.R. rulebook, he received the following reply from Euston.

In future no Welshman to be appointed to a responsible post who cannot read and write English, and the men now employed for whom the rule book is proposed to be translated to be informed that they must learn to speak and read English to entitle them to remain in the service.'

2. Cross over the bridge and notice the cottages to the right (C) and the caravan site to the left.

C. This is River View Terrace; the only terrace built on the 'wrong' side of the railway line. The caravans occupy land that had previously been part of a farm, Glanmorfa, before the railway arrived in the mid-nineteenth century. The farm continued but as the railway grabbed more and more of the farmland, by compulsory purchase, the farm became less and less viable. When the last land-demand arrived the old farmer became very depressed and died one month later. The family were convinced that the loss of his farm meant the loss of his will to live.

3. Continue down the track until you reach the service road, and look at (D).

D. This soulless place is the new Tre-marl Industrial Estate. Previously this huge area was shared by three concerns: the Glanmorfa farmland; an extensive and lively railway yard; and the Junction Brick Works. Until recent years the tall chimneys of the brickworks were a familiar local landmark. In winter, tramps would come from miles around to share the warmth of the kilns. At haymaking time the brickworkers would often help the farmer at Glanmorfa with the harvest, even though they had already put in a very tiring shift.

Turn left along the road, and you soon come to a level crossing (E).

E. This is the Conwy Valley line which continues to Blaenau Ffestiniog. The original proposals for this line were to leave the mainline at Conwy and run down the western bank of the river, via Dolgarrog and Trefriw. The eastern bank route was eventually preferred, and opened to Llanrwst in 1863, extended to Betws-y-coed in 1867 and Blaenau Ffestiniog in 1879.

4. Continue along this road until you can see an old stone viaduct (F) in front of you.

F. This is Pensarn Viaduct which was constructed as part of the original Chester to Holyhead Railway project. The viaduct carried the old road across, what was then, the new railway. Over the years the arches were filled in giving the appearance of an embankment. When the road was widened in recent years the revelation of these attractive arches came as a complete surprise.

5. Walk up to this road, turn left and continue across the viaduct. Turn left at the corner, pausing alongside the first terrace of houses (G).

G. This area used to be called Pensarn, and these were Pensarn Cottages; but as the fields of the Junction filled with buildings, Pensarn lost its separate identity. The cottages became known as Railway Terrace, and the dominance of the railway is clear from the listing of the professions followed by the residents of the years before the First World War. There was an engine driver, a railway fireman, two porters, six platelayers, a storeman and two bricklayers. Next door to the terrace could be found Hillier's Conway Valley Toffee and Sweet works.

Now look across the road at the Methodist chapel (H).

H. The Methodist chapel, chapelhouse and Bron Heulog all belong to the early days of the Junction, but earlier in the nineteenth century the Royal Oak public house had occupied the site. Before it became a builders merchants Bron Heulog served for many years as the Marl Private Hotel, but the croquet lawns and tennis courts have now disappeared below mountains of gravel and sewer pipes.

Next door is a derelict factory (I).

I. The Hotpoint Factory used to be the biggest employer for miles around and its closure was a devastating blow to the local economy. The building is huge and continues beyond this facade, along Narrow Lane. The site was originally built to manufacture aircraft components

THE HOTPOINT SUPERMATIC

The Supermatic is made at Hotpoint's works at Llandudno Junction. Conway is justifiably proud of it. It has everything a woman has ever wanted in a washing machine.

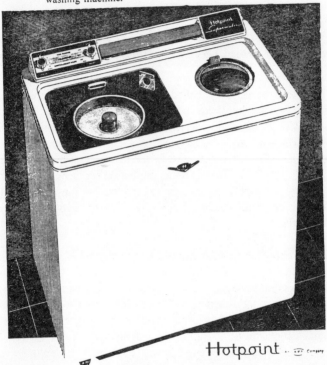

Hotpoint

during the Second World War. In 1947 the Bristol Aeroplane Company leased the factory to the International Refrigeration Company (part of A.E.I.) to produce industrial refrigeration equipment. By 1950 the name had changed to 'Hotpoint' and the fridges had switched to Peterborough (where they were made by another A.E.I. factory). This site went over to producing sewing machines, but soon began to specialise in washing machines. The breakthrough came in 1958 with its famous 'Hotpoint Countess'.

Hotpoint put a lot of money into the factory which now occupied nearly a quarter of a million square feet, and was being described as : 'A showpiece amongst the factories of Europe'. For many years production lines were running day and night. But as Britain gradually lost its market share in the nineteen eighties and nineties, closure became inevitable.

6. As you walk back along Conwy Road towards the Station, on each side of the road you will notice many dead and dying shops (J), pause for thought when you reach the railway station.

J. The commercial heart of Llandudno Junction is in long term decline. Prosperity came with the railway, and disappeared with the motor car. As we continue our walk by exploring the bridging of Afon Conwy it is worth considering how much the improvements in road communications brought work and services to this area (the traditional justification), and how much it simply enabled companies to close local facilities by sourcing from further away in the North of England.

7. Take the Old Conwy Road to the left; pass under the flyover and continue until you reach 'Collinge Antiques' (K).

K. This building served for many years as a Fyffes banana warehouse.

Continue but pause where the road turns to the right (L).

L. The Conwy Road used to turn to the left here and cross the Llandudno branch line over a level-crossing rather than the existing flyover. The level-crossing was a focal point of activity in the national rail strike of 1911, when Union men gathered here and successfully stopped the Llandudno Mail train. Windows were broken, telegraph wires were cut and troops, said to be armed with ball cartridges, rushed to the scene. There were no serious injuries here, but at Llanelli Station in South Wales, troops shot two demonstrators dead. Railwaymen at the Junction also showed great solidarity during the General Strike of 1926, when they refused bribes of £50 each that were offered to run the 'Club Train' to enable wealthy commuters to get to their businesses in the North of England.

8. Pass under the second flyover and ascend the stairs to the footway alongside the road. Notice the traffic on the main road below (M), the bus and coach station (N) to the right, the row of cottages adjacent to the railway (O); and the little road beyond the cottages (P).

M. The Conwy tunnel was officially opened in October 1991. The traffic passes under the river through huge concrete tubes. These six tubes, each measuring 130 yards in length, 26 yards in width and 12 yards in height, were cast at the riverside whilst a huge trench was excavated from the river bed. The tubes were floated out, dropped into place in the trench, and joined end to end. The trench was then filled, bringing the river bed, more or less, back to its original level.

N. The bus and coach station to your right was built in 1924 for the Royal Blue Bus Company, and later taken over by Crosville who have now become 'Arriva'. Notice also the building with the round corner windows and tower, opened in the nineteen twenties as a futuristic showroom for the North Wales Power Company.

O. The row of cottages adjacent to the Llandudno branch line were built to house railway-workers. They remind us of the previous dominance of the railway in moving both people and freight. As late as the nineteen fifties, 100,000 people booked tickets from the Junction every year; more than 100 passenger trains and 25 freight trains were served every day; and more than 130 people were directly employed at the station.

P. Just beyond the end of the railway terrace, a small road runs off to the right. This is Ferry Farm Road and although nothing remains beyond the name, it serves to remind us of a time before the tunnel or any of the bridges allowed travellers to cross Afon Conwy, and remain dry. A regular ferry service operated here from at least the thirteenth century. The Conwy Ferries did, however, have a dreadful reputation. The weather was often adverse, and the ferrymen were commonly abusive and always mercenary. When Roger Fenton passed this way in the early eighteenth century he experienced; 'the most unexampled and savage insolence from the Ferrymen'. When an eighteenth century tourist, Mr Hutton, objected to the way his horses were whipped onto the ferry, he observed that for all its effectiveness he might just as well have addressed the boat as the boatmen. On Christmas Day 1806 an event occurred here that was to hasten the call for the construction of a road bridge, and for the demise of this historic ferry service. When the Mail Coach arrived from Chester the regular ferrymen had already departed to collect their Christmas boxes and begin carousals. The water was far from calm and several passengers refused to board the ferry, returning to the Ferry Farm Hotel. As the ferry reached mid-passage the wind got up and it was proving difficult to maintain control; panic set in and the boat overturned. Rescue was attempted but only two were saved, whilst thirteen drowned.

9. Turn now and walk across the modern road bridge as far as the first steps. There are wonderful views to all sides. Go down to the promenade level, and continue in the direction of Conwy until you can go no further (Q). You get a good view of the second road bridge (R) from here.

Q. You are now standing on an island called Ynys Tŵr y Castell. At least you would have been standing on an island before it was joined to the eastern bank by the construction of an embankment more than a third of a mile long, in 1825. As you can see, there is no bridge across at this level, but from here you can better see the structure of the second road bridge.

R. Opened in 1958 and originally designed by H.W. FitzSimons, who died before the bridge was complete, this bridge marks the beginnings of the mass ownership of cars. By helping to bring even more cars into the narrow walled town of Conwy, it created more problems than it solved. Within two years of the opening, plans were being put forward for further bigger bridges. Proponents of such schemes argued that traffic must be able to flow along the coast to promote the economy of North Wales. Traffic samples were made to establish the importance of removing this bottleneck for the free flow of through traffic. The results proved very surprising. The great majority of traffic was local; not on its way to Holyhead or Chester; but beginning and ending its journey within the boundaries of Conwy and Colwyn Bay. Journeys which could have been served by a free, comfortable and reliable bus service. This might have proved a cheaper and more desirable alternative to another river crossing, because the tunnel cost around £200 million pounds.

10. Now walk back a little to the bottom of the slope, which you then ascend to reach the roadway. Continue to the Conwy end of the bridge. Now you must choose. The recommended route is to cross and walk back over Telford's suspension bridge (S), but this will cost you about a pound (National Trust members walk free). If you prefer to view the bridge from a distance, return the way you came.

S. Conwy Castle is a World Heritage Site, and Telford's Suspension Bridge is a complementary masterpiece. Designed to look like a mediaeval drawbridge to the castle, it succeeds admirably. No useless ornament, it served as the only road crossing into Conwy for one hundred and thirty-two years. Although the decking has been renewed, the chains are still original. Before Telford could build the bridge he had the massive task of constructing the 660 yard embankment, which was to serve as the approach road. The embankment alone took three years to build. The impetus for the whole project had been twofold: firstly the Act of Union with Ireland in 1801 had reinforced the importance of convenient transport links; the other push came from the unsatisfactory nature of the existing Conwy ferry. Ironically, although the swift passage of the mails from Liverpool to Ireland had been a key factor in the building of the bridge, within two months of its opening on the 1st July 1826 the mails were transferred to the Liverpool/Dublin steamships. Even greater irony allows Conwy to take pride in the survival of this historic gem, for on 19th January 1965 the electors of the town voted by a ratio of 3 to 2 to demolish it! Where you hand over your toll for crossing the Telford bridge was the original toll-keeper's cottage. Your fee now includes the right to have a look around inside. The rooms are furnished in a late Victorian style.

Whether you have inspected Telford's suspension bridge from near or far, it's now time to consider the railway bridge (T).

T. This railway bridge was designed and built by Robert Stephenson. Unfortunately the engineering success of this bridge is its architectural downfall. The original idea was to suspend the metal railway-carrying tubes from chains that were slung from the immense catellated towers. When they tested the strength of these tubes by leaving over-loaded freight trains standing inside for a while, they found that the tubes stood up so well, they could dispense with the chain supports altogether. As a result we are left with a dull, heavy-looking, structure that is unrelieved by the tracery of chains or the visible movement of trains. Interestingly, when trains got so heavy by the end of the nineteenth century that the bridge did begin to sag a bit, they still declined to fit chain suspension. Instead they decided to effectively reduce the span from 400 feet to about 310 feet, by inserting massive cast-iron pillars under each end of the tubes.

11. Walk back across the river towards the Junction, and compare the distinctly different bridge designs as you go. To me, Telford's bridge adds rather than detracts from the beauty of the scene. Retrace your steps until you almost reach the station but, instead, cross to the Old Station Hotel (U) for refreshments.

U. THE OLD STATION HOTEL

Address: Conwy Road, Llandudno Junction (Tel. 01492-581259)

Refreshment: Range of bar meals and restaurant service

Description: This is really the new station hotel as the old Junction Hotel served the previous Llandudno Junction station. Both have been demolished but their replacements are still full of character. The Old Station Hotel retains some of the atmosphere of the golden age of rail travel. Lord Woolton, the wartime minister of food, retained a bedroom here for the duration of the war, considering it far enough from colleagues in Colwyn Bay but convenient for frequent rail trips down to London. Even Princess Margaret has dropped in, but only to use the ladies toilets, on the 29th January 1966.

Rambling around Rhos

Walk Number:	Seven
Distance:	Three miles
Terrain*:*	Easy, level, paved mostly along the promenade
Start:	Llandrillo-yn-Rhos (Rhos-on-Sea) Golf Clubhouse, Penrhyn Bay
Finish:	Circular
Transport*:*	Bus 14 or 16 at 30 minute intervals

Introduction:

We begin our walk near Rhos-on-Sea (Llandrillo-yn-Rhos) golf club in an area with a history that may be little appreciated, but that is nonetheless fascinating. The very name Rhos-on-Sea is a marker of social change; of the power of English commerce to supplant ancient Welsh culture. Yet, as we shall see, these same commercial pressures are themselves constantly changing. What has happened to Rhos Pier, the Picture Playhouse or the Budget Tollgate? Was America really discovered from Rhos-on-Sea? Step right this way please . . .

The Walk and Points of Interest:

1. Starting from the golf clubhouse (A), on Glan-y-môr Road.

A. Llandrillo-yn-Rhos golf club was originally developed from the farmhouse and land of Rhydycerrig Gwynion farm. When the club opened on 1st January 1900, it offered membership to gentlemen for two guineas; ladies and 'Honourable Members' for one guinea; and 'juveniles' for ten shillings and sixpence. The farmhouse was modernised and extended to form the clubrooms, and the facilities included stabling for horses and bicycles. The golf course really hit the headlines on the 10th August 1910 when the first aeroplane ever to land in Wales came down, just 100 yards from the clubhouse. The club secretary apparently ran out to greet the aviator, Robert Lorraine, clad

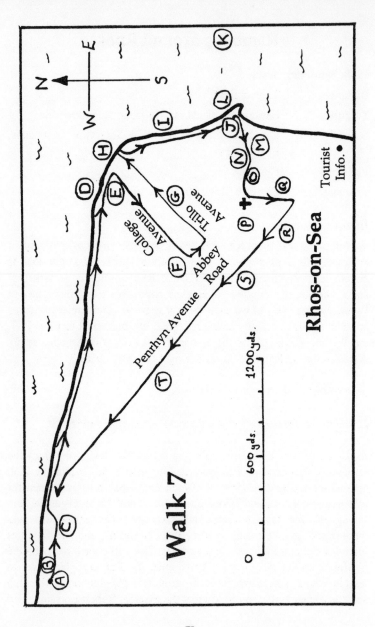

Walk 7

Rhos-on-Sea

Penrhyn Avenue

College Avenue

Trillo Avenue

Abbey Road

Tourist Info.

0   600 yds.   1200 yds.

only in pyjamas, and with toothbrush in hand. Lorraine had planned to land in Holyhead in preparation for an attempt to cross the Irish Sea, but adverse weather forced him down. Word spread rapidly, and within an hour crowds appeared to see the Farman Biplane, with its Gnome engine and its foolhardy pilot. Before noon extra trams had been laid on to convey hundreds more to witness this historic event. When he took off later that day he blamed the fatigue caused by dealing with such huge crowds for the fact that he flew off in completely the wrong direction, but that's another story . . .

at this point there used to be a gate across the road (B).

B. This was The Budget Tollgate, erected in 1908 by the well known local figure and landowner, William Horton. Like many wealthy people, Horton's main reaction to Chancellor Lloyd-George's introduction of Old Age Pensions was to worry that it might result in costing him more in taxes. When Lloyd-George rather flippantly said that he would probably rob someone's nest egg to finance pensions, Horton decided he would introduce his own form of local taxation to cover his anticipated tax increase, and the Budget Toll was born. This roadway was then owned by Horton, and he even charged a penny to push a pram along here. When Horton sold the road to the tram company in 1911 they continued to charge a toll, which was only abolished in 1963 when it was purchased by Llandudno and Colwyn Bay councils and at last given a decent surface. Sadly they also demolished the little toll-house.

2. Continue along Glan-y-môr Road until you notice a large, rather unusual, colonial style building (C) on your right.

C. This is Odstone which has a plaque in the garden claiming that, in 1170, Prince Madog sailed from a harbour here and landed in Mobile Bay, Alabama beating Columbus by 322 years. There is some evidence that a harbour existed here previously, built around the estuary of Afon Ganol. It has been suggested that the stonework forming the rockery at Odstone could be fragmentary evidence of a harbour, or at least a culvert or bridge over a more substantial Afon Ganol. Massive stone walls were also seen in 1907, when a new sewer outfall was being constructed half a mile out to sea from this spot. A lawsuit of 1687 refers to a river mouth or creek on the marsh here, where ships of 20 or 30 tons could find shelter from storms. The main problem with accepting the existence of a harbour here seems to be a Report of the Justices of the Peace For Denbighshire, 1578, which states quite explicitly that there was no trace of a harbour between Conwy and Rhuddlan. As for the role of Madog in discovering America, over the years, much spice was added to that story by claims of the discovery of a tribe of Welsh-speaking native Americans. Unsurprisingly this seems even more difficult to establish.

Cross over and walk along the promenade. Continue until you come to some public toilets, and notice the massive sea defences (D).

D. Early twentieth century pictures of Penrhyn Bay show a far more unspoilt, picturesquely natural looking coastline with a shingle beach, many rock pools, and many happy holiday makers. Unfortunately nature also produced fierce storms, and large sections of the shore were regularly swept away. There were many partial attempts to stabilise the coastline but, eventually, it was deemed necessary to erect the massive coastal defences you can see now. The toilets stand on the site of lime kilns, built to produce lime for the construction of the first sea wall erected here in the 1890's. The modern sea defences may not be picturesque, but it would have looked a whole lot worse if one particular idea proposed at the end of the war had been executed. The plan was to buy fifty army-surplus tanks, park them on the shore between Rhos and Penrhyn Bay, and fill them with concrete to be left as a rusting breakwater.

Look across the road at the houses almost on opposite corners of College Avenue (St Michael's [E] is one house from the corner, on the left).

E. Both St Michael's Nursing Home and The Breakers were built in the 1930's as daring examples of the 'Modernist Movement'. Whilst they are architecturally exciting, problems inevitably arise from the characteristic incorporation of flat roofs.

Cross and walk down College Avenue, noticing the large building at the end (F), on the right.

F. On the right is the eponymous college, built as a boys preparatory school by a Mr Glover. This later became a fee-paying Catholic School which closed in recent years. It stands empty; another characterful local landmark awaiting demolition.

Turn left and return up Trillo Avenue; stop at number 6 (G) on the right.

G. Number 6 and number 4 (which is tucked slightly into the background) are both listed for their architectural merit. Built in 1932 and 1931 respectively, they are good examples of the work of architects North and Padmore of Llanfairfechan. North wrote two excellent books on the old buildings of Snowdonia; one on cottages, and the other on Churches, John Betjeman was a great admirer of North's work and compared his influence to that of Voysey in England and Rene Mackintosh in Scotland. CADW refer to North as the 'outstanding Arts and Craft architect of his age in Wales'.

Continue ahead and return to the seafront; descend the slope to your left to the old church (H).

H. St Trillo's Chapel was established by a sixth century Celtic missionary who, like Tudno, came to evangelise Wales. Obviously a reliable water supply was a priority, even for a hermit, and the chapel probably originates from the simple shelter Trillo would have built to protect himself, and the well he had dug for himself. That well is said to still exist below the present altar. Later the chapel was taken on by the Cistercian Monks from the nearby abbey, and its religious significance continued and developed. They may well have been responsible for rebuilding the chapel in stone. For many years water from St Trillo's well was used to baptise people for miles around, but in the nineteenth century it fell into sad disrepair until William Horton acquired the Rhos estate in 1896 and set about renovating the chapel. Services are still occasionally held in the chapel, and there is room for six worshippers inside.

3. Continue walking along the sea front (I) and consider the activities of many years ago.

I. Less sanctified activities were long carried out along this shore. In 1761 two Customs Officials, Robert Lloyd and David Jones, came upon smugglers at work here. Contraband was being unloaded from a sailing wherry and brought ashore by two smaller boats. A large crowd was waiting with horses, ready to carry off their illicit duty-frees. Although the smugglers escaped, a hoard of contraband tea was discovered later. Locals were also in trouble for harvesting God's bounty of salvage. In 1820 when the sloop Mary Catherine was driven ashore here and subsequently plundered, the entire congregation of the local Methodist chapel was disciplined for robbing the wreck.

4. Proceed to the semi circle of shops on the front; this was the pierhead (J).

J. Rhos Pier was opened on 11th April 1895. It had been bought secondhand by William Bostock, having originally been sited opposite the Villa Marina in Douglas, Isle of Man. Bostock was a Liverpool merchant who had bought a lot of land in the parish of Llandrillo, and had determined to develop it into a commercial resort. When he died in February 1895 his estate was bought by William Horton, a Birmingham businessman, who continued and enhanced Bostock's ambitious plans. Horton's first act was to ignore the traditional Welsh name and promote the developing resort under the more attractive, to English ears, name of Rhos-on-Sea. Ignoring protests that stretched as far as Parliament, his scheme prevailed. In 1900 Horton launched the Colwyn Bay and Liverpool Steamship Co. Ltd which operated a regular service from here to Llandudno, Menai and Liverpool. Although Colwyn Bay's pier looked more substantial it was only a pleasure pier and, unlike Rhos, could not berth steamers. During the Second World War the Home Guard cunningly thwarted the Nazi efforts to invade Rhos by removing most of the planking from the pier. After further storm damage in March 1953, the council voted by two votes for demolition which was carried out the following year. The small museum building is the original pier ticket office.

If the tide is out you may be able to see spot the remains of a wreck (K) a few hundred yards out and slightly to the left of the original pierhead.

K. These are the remains of the Rhosneigr, a steamship that sank on 20th July 1908. Only a month earlier it had been sold by Horton's C.B. & L. Steamship Company to a Captain Walter Hawthorn of Rhyl. Earlier in the day the Rhosneigr had collected eighty passengers from Llandudno and was scheduled to pick up a further seventy-five from Rhos Pier for the return trip to Blackpool. Approaching Rhos the captain heard a sudden grinding noise from below the waterline and saw water pouring in. He tried to reach the pier but, realising he couldn't quite make it, he ran her aground about two hundred yards from the shore. Everyone was rescued but the cause of the sinking was never adequately explained. Part of the skeleton of the hull and the framework of the paddles are identifiable at low tides.

Now look a little nearer to the shore and you might be able to spot a long, low stone causeway running out from the shore (L).

L. This is the stone base of the Rhosfynach fish weir which operated here for about a thousand years. The idea of these structures was to form a huge funnel into which fish could swim at high tide. The mouth of the weir would be left high and dry as the tide receded and the fish would be left floundering on the beach to be carried off in carts. The foundations of the Rhos weir were of local stone, with a six foot high wattle fence erected on top to allow the water out but keep the fish in. A parliamentary act of 1861 demanded that all such weirs be removed unless it could be proven that they had existed before Magna Carta. The longevity of this weir was established and it was permitted to continue. Possibly established by St Trillo and certainly operated by Cistercian Monks in the middle ages, the weir continued to be commercially effective into this century. Ten tons of mackerel were taken on one tide in 1907, and on another occasion 35,000 herring were left high and dry. The weir proved an attraction and entertainment for visitors too. It was inevitably described in Victorian guidebooks, and the more unusual catches were displayed locally. In 1864 this included a 200lb sturgeon, and the following year an eight foot shark. A photograph of the first survives, but although the shark was reportedly stuffed its present whereabouts are unknown. Similarly lost is 'Jack the Canine Fisher'. The Victorian owner of the fishweir swapped a sack of potatoes for Jack, described as an 'otter-terrier', with the crew of a Prussian schooner that had called into the bay to take on rations. Crowds would regularly gather to watch Jack swim out and retrieve salmon trapped in the weir, before the tide had fully retreated. Jack finally expired after a victorious, though ill-chosen struggle, with a shark. He is said to be preserved as an object of the taxidermist's art, proudly wearing the silver collar presented by public subscription to: 'Jack, the celebrated dog fisher . . . October, 1868', but who knows where? The weir was allowed to fall into disrepair during the First World War, and even its foundations are now difficult to discern.

5. Continue a little further and then cross over the road, passing the Rhos Abbey Hotel (M).

M. The Rhos Abbey Hotel, and its near neighbours, were some of the first buildings to be erected on the seafront here, in the 1860's *Old Price* observed that:

Along this expanse of turf at Rhos one has thought fit to erect a set of lodging houses and a hotel in which the spirit and the letter of ugliness are carried out but too faithfully by an architect who if his own handiwork be not the death of him will surely live to see them pulled down as a nuisance.

The hotel survived, and was enlarged and given a facelift in 1898.

6. *Continue to our refreshment stop, Rhosfynach (N) and the gardens (O) set just behind the hotel.*

N. RHOS FYNACH

Address: Rhos Promenade (tel. 01492-548185)

Refreshments: Excellent range of snacks, meals and drinks.

Description: A wonderful hostelry. Rhosfynach's origins lie with a purchase of land by Ednyfed Fychan in 1230, and its subsequent transfer of ownership to the monks of Aberconwy. This was some sort of house or hostelry for the monks who would also have maintained the holy well and chapel of St Trillo, and obtained food and probably some income from the fish weir. In later years Rhosfynach fell into gross decline. For a while it was a particularly characterful but decrepit cafe. Then it passed into the ownership of Colwyn Bay Borough Council who were already allowing the historic fish weir to fade into oblivion. They decided that Rhosfynach, which was officially listed as a Building of Historic and Architectural Importance, should be demolished. Fortunately it was saved and now operates as a very attractive and successful inn.

O. For nearly fifty years the gardens outside Rhosfynach, and behind the Rhos Abbey Hotel, housed the Llandrillo-yn-Rhos open air swimming pool. Opened on Friday, 28th July 1933 by Jack Petersen, reigning heavyweight boxing champion of Great Britain, this was not just a pool but an entertainment complex. There was a cafe, and twice weekly a 'Crazy Nights' variety entertainment. It got harder to attract customers and in 1966 the Council acquired the complex and considered many schemes for enhancing or converting the facilities. There were plans for an 'Ice Palace'; 'Treasure Island'; and an indoor bowls centre. All were to no avail, and the pool was demolished leaving no sign to indicate that it ever existed.

7. When you leave Rhosfynach, turn right and continue to the church (P) ahead.

P. The United Reform Church, opened on the 3rd December 1930, is a late architectural flower of the Arts and Craft Movement. Designed by Bradshaw, Gas and Hope of Bolton the excellent exterior is complimented by the beautiful panelling, lovely central pulpit, and light oak choir stalls of the interior. It is interesting to note that the school room and caretaker's cottage are at the other end of Colwyn Avenue (you will walk past them in a minute). The church was intended to be built there as well, but the trustees were compelled to sell the intended site to the Council for road widening.

8. Continue along Colwyn Avenue until you reach the junction with Penrhyn Avenue. Notice the Co-op shop (Q) on your left.

Q. This wonderfully pretty little frontage was the Rhos Picture Playhouse Cinema opened on Saturday, 11th April 1914, after a preliminary skirmish with the local magistrates about the safety of the building. The architect was the well known S. Colwyn Foulkes, and the original manager was Harold Hill. The cinema held 500, and was beautifully finished with decorative cornicing and oak panelled walls. During most of its lifetime it was owned and managed by Sydney Frere who had previously been a singer and comedian with Catlin's Pierrot Show.

If you look over to your left you will notice second-hand car showrooms (R).

R. In the nineteenth century this was a boatyard; later functioning for many years as The Rhos County Garage: 'The Largest Garage on the North Wales Coast'.

9. Continue along Penrhyn Avenue, passing the cricket ground (S).

S. Rhos-on-Sea Cricket Club Ground opened on the 10th May 1924. The first match was Denbighshire versus Caernarfonshire with Lord Colwyn bowling the first ball. The club is still thriving and continues to host regular County and Exhibition Matches.

10. Continue until you reach a large road haulage garage operated by Lynx Transport (T).

T. This was the main transport depot of the much lamented Llandudno and Colwyn Bay Electric Tramway 1907-1956. Trams from Llandudno ran down Glan-y-môr Road, turned into Penrhyn Avenue past the depot, along the front and then onto Cayley Promenade, and continued on into Colwyn Bay *via* Whitehall Road. By the nineteen fifties buses were proving more popular, and after the last tram ran on Saturday, 24th March 1956 the tram company itself ran a fleet of six double-decker buses between Llandudno and Colwyn Bay and these were then garaged here in the depot. Notice the single storey building to the left of the garage, 'Marval Mechanical Services'; this used to be the Tramway Offices, but the frontage was more ornate in those days. Originally a cycle shop, the building had also previously served as an Ebenezer Mission Hall and a working man's drinking club.

11. Continue along Penrhyn Avenue and Glan-y-môr Road for four hundred yards to return to your starting point.

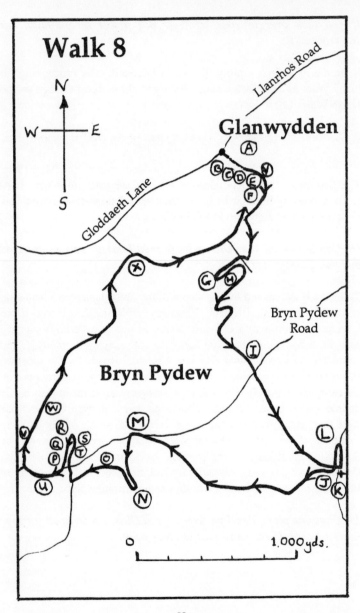

Walk 8

N
W — E
S

Llanrhos Road

Glanwydden

Gloddaeth Lane

Bryn Pydew Road

Bryn Pydew

0   1,000 yds.

A Tale of Two Villages

Walk Number:	Eight
Distance:	Four miles
Terrain:	Moderately strenuous with some steep, slippery slopes and overgrown paths
Start:	Where Llanrhos Road meets Ffordd Glanwydden
Finish:	Circular
Transport:	Bus 12, 13, 15; 20 minute intervals; half-mile walk to start point (from mini-roundabout on Llanrhos Road to Glanwydden)

Introduction:

As towns grow they tend to incorporate the smaller villages and hamlets on their outskirts. From its origins on the Great Orme Llandudno has spread out to embrace Nantygamar, Pantywennol, Bodafon and onwards to Deganwy and Penrhyn Bay. The old agricultural and quarrying area to the south-east of Creuddyn has managed to retain some of its separate, independent character. Yet, even here, the communities of Glanwydden and Pydew have been transformed since the war. Village life is now very different. A trip to Llandudno is no longer an event. It's no longer possible to be born, educated, entertained, employed and married without leaving the comfort of one's own village.

The Walk and Points of Interest:

1. Walk down Ffordd Glanwydden until you come to the old windmill (A) (that has no sails).

A. The mill has a keystone dated 1704 above the main door, but this relates to a subsequent rebuilding. The earliest reference to a windmill here appears in a lease granted to William Salesbury of Glanwydden at the end of the sixteenth century. This makes the Glanwydden Mill rather older than Hen-dŵr, the mill tower above Gloddaeth. Hen-dŵr seems to have lost its sails in the early part of the nineteenth century whilst Glanwydden's were retained until the latter part of the century. Glanwydden's more accessible approach undoubtedly enabled it to outlast Hen-dŵr but, inevitably, it fell victim to the same economic forces that sealed the fate of every other windmill. Farmers were turning *en masse* from grain production to stock rearing because imported grain had so depressed prices. Consequently there was much less local demand for the mills' services. The invention of the steam engine also enabled huge, steam powered, steel roller-mills to produce vast quantities of much finer flour at much lower cost. The village baker could get white flour delivered from a Liverpool mill at a cheaper cost than locally stoneground, wholemeal flour. As white bread was immediately preferred as more civilised and sophisticated, progress killed off our first village victim. The Glanwydden Mill was gutted and served as a cowshed. The decaying remains stood for more than a century to remind villagers of a bygone industry, before being sold in the nineteen eighties and rather sympathetically converted into a dwelling.

Notice the building on the opposite side of the road, on the right (B).

B. For many years this was a village shop. Latterly it was Pickering's Grocers, Bakers and Confectionery Store. They did the baking themselves, and also delivered locally. Car ownership killed their trade as villagers chose to drive to bigger shops in town, and save a few pence.

To the left are the dwellings (C).

C. Now three cottages, this used to be a pub and a shop. In the nineteenth century the two cottages on the left formed the *King's Head.* In 1880 the licensee was John Edwards. 'The Old Shop' next door lingered on into the nineteen fifties selling a small range of sweets and cigarettes, and run by Mrs Hughes.

2. Continue past Pendyffryn Cottages to a house set back at an angle to the road (D).

D. This is thought to have been a public house called *The Sun,* but it had become a private house by the early years of the nineteenth century.

Notice an extremely attractive stone cottage (E) a few steps further along.

E. Penstore has a blocked-up opening facing the road; this was a sort of window with shutters. It was another of the early village shops.

3. Notice the Queen's Head (Y), across the road, this will be our refreshment place on our return. Continue on, turning right at the corner and stop outside the chapel (F).

F. The Ainon Welsh Baptist Chapel dates from 1840 but was founded in 1799. The single storey section on the left is the schoolroom. The name of the Chapel alludes to the proximity of the stream that flows through the village, Nant Wydden. To the faithful of earlier generations that were immersed in the Bible, Ainon was familiar as a part of the Holy Land with an abundance of natural water. If you look over the wall next to the chapel you can see the stream, which is now culverted through much of the village where previously it flowed openly. A long serving minister here was the eloquent preacher and stirring political orator, James 'Spinther' James. We shall soon visit his grave on our walk where I will tell more about him. Notice the attractive, blacksmith-made iron gate.

4. Continue along the road, noticing the delightful scene on your left where the ducks are paddling in the stream by the roadside. About fifty yards past the ducks, turn down a footpath on the left over the stream. Cross the field diagonally and, after about 200 yards, emerge onto a minor paved road. Turn right and continue for a few paces until you see an attractive set of plain iron gates with a metal kissing gate to the right. These gates look like the work of the same man who made those of the chapel, probably at the local smithy which we will visit later. Go through this gate and continue along the grass lane until you realise that you are in what may be the most overgrown graveyard you have ever seen. You are looking for the tallest upright memorial on your left (G) – when you locate it, try to read the inscription on the other side.

G. This is the grave of James 'Spinther' James (1837-1914) of Glanwydden Chapel. Spinther was active in all the great issues of the Victorian period; the social and political as well as the religious. His main literary output was devoted to the research and recording of Welsh history and culture in its widest sense. At the time of his death he had been working on a 'History of Creuddyn and Modern Llandudno'. Spinther had become minister at Glanwydden in 1870, and although he gave up his ministry in 1888 in order to devote himself to his writing, he continued to preach on Sundays and other special occasions at Ainon. He was very politically involved in local issues too; he published a paper criticising the ineptitude of Llandudno's Improvement Commissionaires; he organised meetings and made speeches strongly denouncing Mostyn's leasehold system; and he gave public encouragement to local farmers that were engaged in the anti-tithe struggle.

5. Retrace your footsteps out of the graveyard, turn right and continue to the houses at the top of the lane. Turn right and walk along the path at the rear of the houses, pause just beyond the last house in the terrace (H) where there is an arched entrance gate.

H. This area is called Ffolt, and this terrace housed workers at the stone quarries on your left. At the turn of the century, stone quarried here was used to build the Grand Hotel in Llandudno. There used to be another building at this end that opened on the 9th July 1877 as the local school, and this slightly crenellated arch was the entrance gate. It was a one-up, one-down affair with infants downstairs, the rest upstairs, and very smelly toilets. Children walked here from as far as Llangystennin and Penrhynside, but only when they weren't required for planting potatoes or getting in the harvest, for this was a poor area. Serious infectious diseases, like diphtheria, tuberculosis, scarlet fever and even typhoid, caused frequent closures and several children died. The poor state of the school building was frequently criticised by Inspectors, and in 1911 it finally closed and the pupils were transferred to the new Glanwydden school. It was used to house German prisoners during, and after, World War One but was badly damaged by fire in 1919. It was finally demolished in the nineteen fifties.

6. Continue along this path for about fifty yards when you should be able to notice the ruins of a masonry structure in the undergrowth on your left; these are the remains of an old lime kiln. Turn left along a path which winds uphill here; you soon pass an old smallholding on your right called Wiga. Continue uphill until you notice an intriguing, half-buried structure (I) in front of you.

I. This is a particularly nice example of the water storage tanks that used to be common in country areas before most houses were directly connected to the mains supply.

7. Cross the road and take the farm track past Tan-y-bryn. Continue south-east to the top of the ridge where you will have reached a height of about 400 ft, with views over the surrounding countryside and along the coastline. Continue towards the trees and, getting a little closer to the field boundary away on your left, you are looking for a rather faint path which descends diagonally through the trees. When you reach a clearing, you notice a stile ahead on the edge of more woodland. Cross here and follow the path down through this rather wonderful woodland, eventually emerging through a short straight, fenced path onto a minor road. Cross to the church (J) and graveyard (K).

J. This is Llangystennin Church which takes its name from Saint

Cystennin, son of Elen o Arfon and Macsen Wledig. It's a lovely romantic spot. The anti-vandal protection on the church windows obscures the details, making it difficult to appreciate the remaining medieval glass. This has long been a place of worship, but the present building largely dates from 1843. This was the church that served the people of the two villages that concern us today, Glanwydden and Pydew, before the Established Church was increasingly eclipsed by non-conformism as the nineteenth century progressed. The religious zeal of local parishioners is apparent in the outcome of a meeting held in the church, in 1814, which resolved that:

> The inhabitants of this neighbourhood taking into consideration . . . the benighted state of the heathens, the truly carnal and sensual doctrines of Mahomet, the gross and absurd impositions of other sects, resolve to . . . sanctify these morally polluted and depraved souls by sending copies of the Bible to every nation on earth.

K. The gravestones record something of the sad decline of local villages. All fairly near to the church are the graves of Margaret Davies, The Shop, Glanwydden (d.1886), James Williams of The Shop, Pydew, Jesse Roberts of The New Shop, Bryn Pydew (d.1881), four memorials commemorating the Roberts family of the Red Lion, Pydew and two dedicated to Elizabeth Jones and William Thomas both of the Swan Inn, Pydew. All are shops or inns that no longer trade.

8. *Leave the churchyard and turn right along the road. After fifty yards or so you should pause in front of Llangystennin Hall (L).*

L. Llangystennin Hall was built in 1638 and was the home of the Lloyd family in the 17th and 18th centuries. In the eighteen hundreds it declined in social status, and was tenanted for a while before being abandoned. In 1905 it was renovated and extended although the original oak beams were preserved in the kitchen, study and bedrooms. It has been sold several times during the twentieth century. In November 1945 it was bought, together with twelve and a half acres of land, by Harold Rees for £5,600. By 1986 the land was down to eight acres, but the price had gone up to £165,000.

9. Retrace your route up through the woods. Do not turn off to left or right, but continue until you finally reach a stile at the edge of the wood. Cross and turn right along the edge of the wood, then take the first turning on the left. Continue along this path until you reach a field gate with a rusting abandoned car alongside. Go through this gate and continue along the green road. After a few hundred yards you notice wonderful views to your left over the head of the Conwy Valley. Continue until you finally emerge, through a field gate, onto a metalled road, and pause here at the edge of Bryn Pydew village with fields on your right (M).

M. The fields on your right were the scene of a dramatic wartime aeroplane crash. On 27th October, 1944 the pilot of a Handley Page Halifax, HR723, began to lose control of the aircraft as it started to ice up at 15,000 feet. Losing height he gave the order for the crew to bale out. They all got out before the plane was down to 5,000 feet and six of them landed safely, but the wireless operator's parachute failed to open and he was killed. The pilotless Halifax spiralled lower until finally ploughing into a cowshed.

10. Bearing slightly to the left, continue along the road for a hundred yards, passing a small church on your right and a recreation ground on your left. When you reach a junction which offers three options, take the immediate left. Walk along this lane, bearing slightly to the left, for about 200 yards when you will see an old white painted farmhouse (N) in front of you.

N. This is Pen-y-bryn Cottage, a substantially unaltered mid-eighteenth century farmhouse. Inside there are original large slate slabs on the ground floor, with wide wooden floorboards upstairs. A public footpath passes through the farmyard so it is possible to also appreciate the traditional range of outbuildings.

11. Retrace your steps a little back along the lane to the point where a lane (O) goes off to the left. Pause here.

O. This lane exemplifies the agricultural side of the village of Bryn Pydew with smallholdings scattered to left and right. Unfortunately, whilst a degree of neglect has preserved the character of Pen-y-bryn, modernisation has removed virtually all the historic value of Baron Hill, which was a typical Welsh crogloft cottage with the upper storey accessible by ladder only.

12. Now take this lane that goes off to the left, and you soon come to a paved minor road. Turn left and descend into the heart of the village of Bryn Pydew. You will notice ahead a bench in the middle of the triangular 'village green', where you can rest. You may well be alone, but years ago this was a vital place with people meeting and greeting, coming and going from the shop, school, chapel or pub which were all around you. Notice the large painted house, Karenza (P); and also buildings (Q), (R) and (S).

P. Karenza, the large painted house, was Mister Evans' shop. He sold everything; postal orders, chicken food, medicine, ham, lemonade; he baked bread on the premises. His shop was a wonderland that is remembered with affection by older villagers. If you preferred, you could have your order delivered by Mr Evans, using his horse and cart. In the days before everything came wrapped in plastic, shops had to store many sacks of basic commodities to be later weighed and wrapped for individual customers. Mr Evans stored his goods next door, in the building which has since been converted into a house called Fieldcroft.

Q. The school was the building end-on to the road, before the chapel. Originally a vestry, in November 1921 this became Bryn Pydew Elementary School. All twenty-one pupils, of various ages, were taught together in the one room classroom. Many villagers remember with special affection Mrs Murray-Williams who taught here for twenty-five years after spending her previous eight years teaching on

Ynys Enlli. In 1965 the school was closed and all the village children, and much of the furniture, was transferred to Glanwydden school.

R. Capel y Bryn was opened in the nineteenth century as a Welsh Calvinistic Chapel. It can accommodate one hundred and sixty people, and even after the Second World War it managed to retain about one hundred and forty members, but in recent years as the old members passed on they were not replaced by youngsters, and chapel attendance fell dramatically. By 1996 there were only about six regular attenders and with great sadness the decision was taken to close the following September.

S. In the nineteenth century the house below you, Islwyn, was run as a pub called The Red Lion.

Notice also the old lamp post (T), now minus the lamp.

T. There used to be three oil street lights in the village. There was one along the main road, now removed; another one near the main road that was recently converted to electricity; and this one. The horizontal crosspiece was for the lamplighter, Griff Jones of Rala (the cottage behind the school), to rest his ladder against.

13. Return to the main road, turn right and soon you notice a single storey cottage (U) set back on the left.

U. This is Granllyn, an eighteenth century cottage which has the distinction of being the last house in Creuddyn to retain its thatched roof, now sadly replaced by slate. Opposite is the old Swan, which also previously served as a public house, before becoming a shop. It continues to provide a basic Post Office service for the village and a small notice in the front window indicates if it is open for business.

14. Continue along the road, soon turning off to the right down Goedlodd Lane. After about 150 yards, notice an old spear-ended metal garden gate (V) alongside the lane on the right, just before you reach the timber bungalow.

V. If you fancy a cup of tea, you are just fifty years too late! In the old days this quiet spot offered a choice of refreshment places. This gate led to the extensive facilities offered by Midacres Tea Gardens. This was run by three sisters called the Misses Bramblin, and as well as a range of refreshments, they also offered tennis courts, bowling and croquet.

15. A little further along the lane, on the right, is Micklebrow (W).

W. This used to be Bryn Awelon Bungalow Cafe. Bryn Awelon was opened as a cafe by Miss Evans in the early years of the century and continued as such into the nineteen fifties, run by Mrs Pillbeam. The cafe was a prefabricated structure made of timber and asbestos. In its latter years the business depended on Llandudno's army of exiled civil servants' predilection for country walks. Mrs Pillbeam would produce mountains of baking in anticipation of crowds of weekend customers. Bad weather meant that, for the next few days, the family could expect scones for breakfast, dinner and tea.

16. A little further ahead you turn left and then right alongside the garden of the pretty, white painted Goedlodd Cottage, and continue through the kissing gate. Here the path may be overgrown but continue downwards, bearing round to the left until you come to a wall. Continue alongside this wall and soon you go through a farm gate into the yard of Cilmeityn Farm. A little further on you go through the field gate on the left, and continue along the right hand edge of the first two fields. Turn left at the far end of the second field, and continue along the field edge again. You are heading for the house you can see over on your left. Cross two ladder stiles and then, turning right, cross the corner of one last field. Go over the stile and you should find yourself standing in front of Yr Efail (X).

X. This was David William's blacksmith's shop. He made the Chapel and burial ground gates we saw earlier. Shoeing a pony here cost three pence, but it was a shilling for a shire. His son, John, continued until the nineteen thirties when mass-production and cars finally destroyed the business.

17. Continue along Lôn yr Efail, and then go left at the junction. This is Waun Road which takes us back to 'The Queen's Head' (Y).

Y. THE QUEEN'S HEAD

Address: Glanwydden Village, tel. 01492-546570.

Food: The food is good but not cheap. Bar meals, restaurant service and an excellent range of wines and beer.

Description: An attractive village pub that is also popular with people from town. The walls are lined with a range of historic photographs of local scenes, and in winter there is a log fire too. Excellent for adults but little provision for young children.

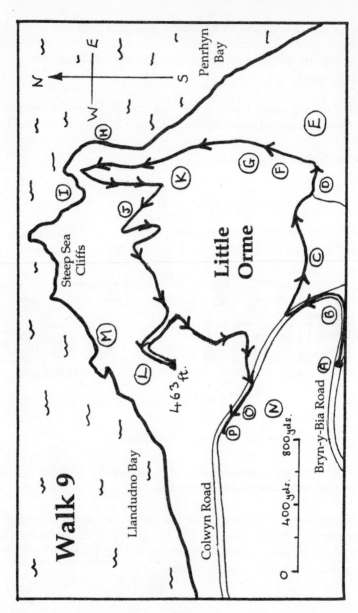

Walk 9

Llandudno Bay

Steep Sea Cliffs

Little Orme

463 ft.

Penrhyn Bay

Colwyn Road

Bryn-y-Bia Road

N · E · S · W

0   400 yds.   800 yds.

Exploring the Little Orme

Walk Number: Nine

Distance: Two and a half miles

Terrain: Includes some rather strenuous, steep walking to the summit; shoes with good grips required

Start: Foot of Penrhynside Hill, Little Orme, Llandudno

Finish: Circular

Transport: Bus 12, 13, 14, 15 or 16 at fifteen minute intervals

Introduction:

Although a similar limestone headland to the Great Orme, the Little Orme has a very different history. Quarrying for stone rather than metal mining has been the most significant activity here, and this quarrying was only developed commercially some thirty years after mining ceased on Y Gogarth. Although much smaller in size than the Great Orme, many consider the view from the top to be superior. On our route to the summit we will also visit the little cove of Porth Dyniewaid, one of the most secluded spots in Creuddyn. In the words of an 1892 guidebook:

> On trip days when the Happy Valley and the Telegraph Station are in full swing . . . a stroll over this comparatively neglected height will specially commend itself to the less exuberant class of visitors.

The Walk and Points of Interest:

1. Notice the single-storey cottage (A) behind, and to the left of, the bus stop which is opposite the foot of Pendre Road.

A. This is Bryn Ifan which has been a three acre smallholding for about three hundred years, with a simple single-storey house existing for most of that period. The present house is much modernised but preserves some character of the original holding. Before the turn of the century this was the major road rather than the one ahead; it connected Llanrhos Parish with Llandrillo. The local legend is that Ifan was an archer who once managed to defend the pass against invaders.

Walk a little further towards the Little Orme until you see another single-storey house (B) on your left.

B. Siop y Roe was a smallholding that also operated as a shop. Between the two wars it also offered refreshments to passers-by.

2. Turn left, walk a little down the hill and cross to the farm lane. Walk along to the farm and ignore the arrow to the left; your right of way is ahead, between the house and the outbuildings (C).

C. This is Ty Ucha, the only remaining farm on the Little Orme. The style of the house suggests that it may have been substantially modernised about 1876 when a new tenant insisted in his lease that necessary repairs be carried out by the Mostyn Estate. The outbuildings have been altered less, and appear to be about two hundred years old. The old stone barn cleverly takes advantage of the sloping ground, with a single storey cowshed at one end and a cartshed with hayloft over at the other. As you pass through the buildings notice, on the left, the old stone pig sties with typical metal gates.

3. Continue along the footpath which was, until the mid nineteenth century, the main approach to the farm. Soon you emerge onto a wider lane, with two old dwellings ahead, both created from Pentre Isa farmstead (D).

D. Pentre Isa farmhouse was built in 1680 but lost much of its character with its conversion into two separate dwellings in the nineteen seventies. If the plans to develop Llandudno as the main ferry port for Ireland, instead of Holyhead, had succeeded, than Pentre Isa would have suffered an earlier and even more severe loss of character. The plan was to take the railway across Pentre Isa land, and through the Little Orme in a tunnel starting near where you are now standing.

The dwelling opposite was converted from one of Pentre Isa's barns.

4. Continue, passing between the two dwellings. Go through the gate and glance over to the right at Penrhyn Beach Estate (E).

E. The modern Penrhyn Beach Estate was developed in the nineteen seventies, largely from the farm land of Pentre Isa.

Continue ahead, and notice the extensive remains of quarrying (F) all around.

F. This is largely the result of the activities of The Little Orme's Head Limestone Company. Their 1889 lease gave quarrying rights over about forty acres of the Little Orme, and by the turn of the century they were employing about eighty people here. The main business was to extract and ship the limestone to the Clyde and Argyll coast ports for use in blast furnaces and the chemical industries. Over the years, the ownership of the company changed and the nature of the quarrying shifted towards extracting and crushing the stone as an ingredient of Portland Cement.

Continue, passing to the right of the huge quarry basin (G).

G. After the war new ideas for the commercial exploitation of the Little Orme were produced. In 1952 it was proposed to create a caravan site here with this basin being filled with water and used as a boating lake. In 1974 the site was proposed as a tip with the basin being filled with rubbish. In 1981 the plan was to fill the basin with the excavations from the new A55 expressway that was then being constructed. Local opposition scuppered all of these schemes.

5. As you pass the end of the basin, wonderful sea vistas open up before you; but do notice the still impressive remains of the old stone quays (H) down to the right.

H. In the early years of the quarry wooden wagons were hauled up and down an incline to the wharf below; but in the early years of the new century this system was replaced with concrete hoppers sited above the wharves, and disgorging directly into ships. The stone simply slid into the hoppers along metal troughs, from the crushing plant above. One thousand ton capacity ships could berth here and be filled in less than an hour.

6. Walk on towards the headland until you can see a little rocky cove (I) far below on the left.

I. The cove is Porth Dyniewaid, and the rocky headland is Trwyn y Fuwch. Notice that the quarry works were effectively screened from Llandudno by this headland. The freehold owners, Mostyn Estates, wanted to maximise their income from their quarry leases here, but they did not want an unsightly quarry to reduce the rental value of their Llandudno properties by spoiling their vistas. The Mostyns therefore included restrictive covenants in their leases which precluded quarrying on the Llandudno side. It was even prohibited to allow smoke to be visible from Llandudno.

This is a wonderful spot, peaceful yet dramatic. It is possible to climb down to the shore here, with care. Turn around and run your eyes along the heights over on your right – can you spot a long grassy slope or incline? This is where we are heading. Make your way over to it and carefully ascend to the top, where you will see a metal winding wheel (J).

J. The incline you just walked up was the trackbed for the trucks whose ascent and decline was controlled by steel cables from the winding wheel. Stone was extracted from the faces you can see; it then descended *via* the incline to the processing and crushing works, and then along the shutes to the hoppers, awaiting shipping. This is a good vantage point for spotting the extensive trackbeds on the lower levels, especially when there are good shadows. You should be able to make out the marks left by the old railway sleepers. The quarry operated its own three foot gauge railway with four steam locomotives. During the

First World War these were driven by women, who also operated the compressed air rock drills and loaded and unloaded the wagons. Although the company were still managing to extract about a quarter of a million tons of stone a year, they ceased all production here at the end of 1931. Many of their buildings remained for some time, with the concrete hoppers only being demolished in 1987.

7. Our route now turns to the left, but do glance down at the extensive level area below. It had another brief life after the quarrying ended when it was taken over by the military (K).

K. In 1917 it was suggested that this site might make a good prisoner of war camp, but the authorities didn't take up the suggestion. In 1941, just ten years after serious quarrying had ended, the War Department requisitioned the site as a practice camp for coastal artillery. The redundant quarry buildings were used, along with a newly erected assortment of Nissen huts and giant guns. Firing would take place night and day, much to the excitement of local childen and the irritation of their parents. As the war drew to a close, the camp was run down and its functions and equipment moved elsewhere. You can still find the concrete bases and metal stanchions left behind, but it is not easy to distinguish these from the remains of the quarry works.

8. Continue upwards following the yellow footpath arrows until you reach a point where a path goes off to the right, following a sort of shallow valley between two peaks, (remember this point, because we shall be returning!). Take this path, and then turn to the left when you see a wooden post ahead. Keep ascending until you reach the triangulation post (L) which soon comes into view.

L. You are now standing at a height of 463 feet. Although it is 200 feet lower than the Great Orme, many consider the view from here to be much finer. There are few obstructions to your view because the grassy slopes drop away so sharply. Perhaps the conspirators who, in 1580, gathered in a cave just 100 feet or so further down these slopes thought that such hazards would ensure their safety. Danger for Father

William Davies existed in the shape of the newly established church, for he was a Catholic priest using the cave to print traitorous Popish tracts. This was the first printing press in Wales. The authorities discovered the cave, probably through an informer, and William Davies was apprehended and sentenced to death. He was informed that the death sentence would be quashed if he renounced Catholicism. He refused and was hung, drawn and quartered at Beaumaris. This cave is located at OS 813825 but you should not attempt to find it as the slope is far too hazardous.

Before you leave this marvellous viewpoint, perhaps another story might serve to illustrate the notoriously dangerous sea cliffs (M) here.

M. In the year 1900 there was a chap working at Pentre Isa Farm called Wiliam Edwards. William was twenty-five and planning to marry Mary Davies who worked at Ty Ucha Farm in Llandudno. Everyone knew that visitors to Llandudno were prepared to pay a shilling each for birds' eggs, and the money would come in handy for the forthcoming wedding. On Saturday evening, 5th May, Mary had been out with William and they parted at nine o'clock the best of friends, promising to meet the next day at Llangystennin at six o'clock. On Sunday morning William set out from Pentre Isa to do some egg collecting. He never arrived for his assignation with Mary. William's body was found wedged between boulders at the foot of the cliffs by a Police Constable Richards. The Constable said it appeared that William had fallen from the top of the Little Orme.

9. If you walk about twenty paces due south ((use map as reference) of the trig. point you should be able to see two small stone houses (N) below you. They have patterned roofs made up of contrasting coloured slates.

N. The land and buildings on the far side of the high limestone wall were all part of the Shimdda Hir Estate. We will presently visit the main house for our refreshments, but first notice the two moderate sized stone houses on the brow of the hill. These were built in about 1880 as staff residences, one for the gardener and the other for the coachman. No longer connected to the big house they are now private residences.

10. Retrace your steps to the point of return (do you remember?). This time, take the path to the right; it may seem a little hidden by the gorse but it is actually part of the official North Wales Path as the waymarked arrows indicate. This is a delightful section which curves as it descends around the hill, finally emerging at the main road through a metal gate. Cross with care, turn right and continue until you reach an entrance drive (O).

O. This driveway serves what was originally the stable block to Shimdda Hir. Like the staff cottages you noticed earlier, it was erected around 1880 when the old Shimdda Hir farmstead was given a complete makeover to replace its agricultural appearance with the character of a 'Gentleman's Residence'. In 1968, along with the main residence it was bought by the Carmelite Religious Order and became St Mary's Convent. The nuns left in 1984 and the stables and main house subsequently passed into separate ownership, with the stables undergoing conversion to a private residence. In 1907, 452 bronze coins of the Roman period were discovered opposite here, on the other side of the road. Workmen were excavating rubble for roadbuilding near the Grand Theatre in Llandudno. By the time someone noticed the coins, they'd already transported some of the rubble. When they had a sift through the roadworks they found over a hundred more coins, so keep your eyes open . . .

11. Continue down the hill until you reach our refreshment place (P).

P. CRAIGSIDE INN

Address: Colwyn Road, Llandudno (tel. 01492-545943)

Refreshments: Good range of bar and restaurant meals with the addition of options designed for children.

Description: The Craigside Inn was originally the big house of the Shimdda Hir Estate. It has been extended and modernised over the years, but the original farmhouse was probably erected in the eighteenth century. Over the years the estate land has varied from ten to thirty acres but now the associated cottages, land and stables have all passed into separate ownership. Whitbread PLC purchased this, the main residence, in the late nineteen eighties. They have created an attractive, comfortable inn with a poor range of beers but an excellent range of play facilities for children.

Three Halls and a Monument

Walk Number: Ten

Distance: Four miles

Terrain: Easy cross-country walking on field paths and through woods, some fairly easy slopes and some mud

Start: Llandudno Junction end of Pabo Lane

Finish: Circular

Transport: Bus 22 or 26, approx. 3 per hour, or train to Llandudno Junction

Introduction:

The scenic delights of the low, wooded hills of Creuddyn have long been appreciated by the gentry. The Halls of Marl, Pabo and Bodysgallen remain as testament to their importance in an earlier age. The subsequent histories and changes in ownership of these grand houses reflect changes that have taken place in our wider society. The natural beauties remain, largely unchanged, providing a walk that is rich in history, natural, social and architectural.

The Walk and Points of Interest:

1. The walk begins very much in the concrete world of the twentieth century, but as you pass under the flyover and walk along Pabo Lane the scene begins to change considerably. Continue for half a mile or so, past several old houses and farms, until you notice an attractive single storey lodge building on your left (A).

A. This is Pabo Lodge, built to serve the Hall which is further along the drive in front of you. In the grandest houses lodgekeepers operated full time to prevent unwanted intruders disturbing the peace of the nobility. In more modest establishments, such as Pabo, the idea was to give the appearance of exclusivity and privacy without the expense.

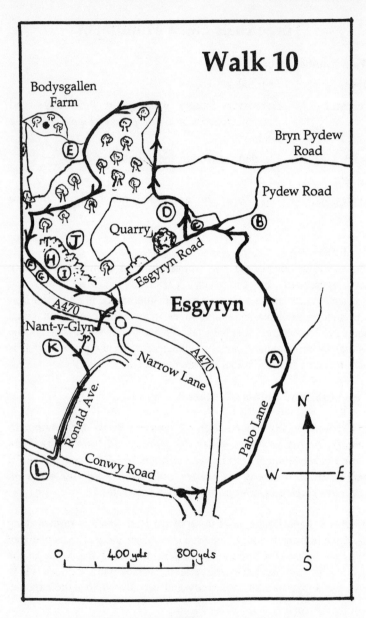

Walk 10

Bodysgallen Farm

Bryn Pydew Road

Pydew Road

E

D

C

B

Quarry

Esgyryn Road

J

H

F

I

G

A470

Esgyryn

Nant-y-Glyn

O

A470

A

K

Narrow Lane

Ronald Ave.

Pabo Lane

L

Conwy Road

N

W —— E

S

0   400 yds   800 yds

Lodges such as these were actually used to house workers, whose real responsibilities lay elsewhere. For the latter part of the Victorian period this lodge provided a home for Richard Roberts who was employed as a gamekeeper rather than a gatekeeper. It has since been sold and is no longer connected with the 'big house'.

2. Walk up the lane by the lodge (not the one to the right), for about five hundred yards. Soon you see the buildings of the old hall (B); pause by the stone archway.

B. Pabo Hall was built towards the end of the seventeenth century, and a grave memorial at Llangystennin Church records the death of John Williams, Gent of Pabo, in 1718. It was not a first class Gentry House, and no continuing lineage was established here. By the early nineteenth century it was let to tenants, with Hugh and Jane Rees in residence, together with a couple of relatives and four servants. Hugh was really a farmer with social aspirations, and liked to describe himself as a 'Landed Proprietor'. Two of his 'servants' were farmhands and the Hall was by then a glorified farmhouse in rather poor repair. Restoration and aggrandizement came with the ownership of Edward Brookes, a widower and Justice of the Peace. He lived here alone, apart from his four domestic servants, in the latter part of the nineteenth century, and spent a lot of money on the old Hall, adding the prominent clocktower in 1884. He was followed by another J.P., Ephraim Wood, who lived here in the first part of the twentieth century. Like so many similar country properties, Pabo was soon to pass into institutional use. During World War Two it served as a regional administrative centre for the control of the prisoners of war that were employed on local farms. After the war it became a country hotel and restaurant (see old advert) before once again becoming a private house.

3. Go through the arch and continue on the path which turns a little to the left. When you meet the paved lane continue downhill for a few yards until, on your right, you spot a stone and concrete affair (C).

*A*fter your walk through
Creuddyn Country a visit to

NON NUMERO HORAS NISI SERENAS

PABO HALL
Hotel

with its charm & *captivating scenery*
will complete your day's enjoyment

Half a mile from Bryn Pydew Village

AFTERNOON TEAS DINNERS ETC.

TEL. LLANDUDNO JUNCTION 811071/81287

C. This stone and concrete 'hut' with letter-box slots in it is a Second World War 'pillbox'. The slots allowed gunners some latitude in firing on enemy troops attemtping an invasion. The elevated position allowed a wide view down the Conwy Valley.

4. Take the footpath which ascends just past the pillbox, soon you notice an obelisk (D) on your left.

D. Many visitors wonder at the origins of this monument. It is, perhaps, a commemoration of Nelson's victory at Trafalgar; possibly it recalls the accession of Queen Victoria in 1837; or maybe her diamond jubilee in 1887. It is none of these. This historic looking needle is no more than an advertisement for the hotel that now occupies Bodysgallen Hall. It was erected in 1992 and immediately caused a storm of protest. Many consider it to be a blot on the landscape, but I feel it is a characterful addition. Many societies have defined their special places with significant structures, and surely this has more merit than the monstrous erections on the summit of the Great Orme or Snowdon, or the electricity and communication pylons on hills all around you.

5. Continue across the field, and when you exit onto a paved lane, turn left and continue downhill for about four hundred yards. Where the road turns sharply to the right, you follow a path which continues straight ahead, across fields for another four hundred yards with the Eastern Covert on your left. You soon reach a well defined path at the north-eastern corner of the woods, where you turn left. Follow the path through this most delightful woodland until you notice the extensive buildings of Bodysgallen Hall (E).

E. It has been claimed that Bodysgallen was originally built by Caswallon, Prince of Gwynedd in the fifth century (Bod Caswallon, home of Caswallon) but some prefer the more prosaic derivation of a place of thistles (ysgallen). It is possible that the central tower section was built as a lookout for possible raids on Conwy Castle, but it seems more likely that Bodysgallen was originally part of the Gloddaeth estate, and became divided with the building of the house at the end of the sixteenth century. It was thus originally in the possession of the Mostyn family. The house and ancilliary buildings have been much added to over the years, but a pleasing architectural consistency has been followed throughout. Bodysgallen is an object lesson in developing, and yet preserving, ancient buildings. This is all the more surprising in a building which must now earn its keep as a commercial concern, for Bodysgallen is now run as a luxurious country hotel. The grounds are equally spectacular with a formal 17th century Dutch garden; an eighteenth century walled rose garden; and a further series of terraces which include a beautiful lily pond. For most of its life Bodysgallen has been in the possession of the Wynne and Mostyn families. During the civil war it was the home of Colonel Hugh Wynne who raised a regiment of cavalry for the Royalist cause, and who participated in the surrender to the Parliamentarians on the 3rd February 1645. In 1766 the estate returned to Mostyn control when Margaret Wynn of Bodysgallen married Sir Roger Mostyn. In 1967 the house finally passed out of the hands of both Wynns and Mostyns, when it was sold at the culmination of a three day grand house sale.

6. Continue along the path until you meet a junction, with paths to the left and right. Turn right and you soon pass, almost imperceptibly, from the old Bodysgallen Estate to the Marl Estate lands. Keep alongside the old stone wall and descend a flight of steps, known locally as Jacob's ladder, to a spring which is surrounded with masonry. The path gets a little confusing here, but you want to head down to your left, in a southerly direction. You cannot go far wrong, and should soon notice a wooden field gate which takes you out onto Marl Lane. Turn left along the lane and notice an old iron, farm-type, gate (F) on the opposite side of the road. A little further along is Marl Farm (G). Opposite, and slightly elevated, is Marl Hall (H).

F. This is an original turnpike gate of about 1820, and of Thomas

Telford's standard design. Turnpikes were privatised sections of roadways where tolls were collected to offset the costs of construction and maintenance, and to make money for the proprietors. It was opposition to the imposition of such payments that provoked the Rebecca Riots of the 1840's, but these were mainly confined to South Wales. This gate is not *in situ,* but would have been bought by a farmer at an auction of the effects of a redundant Turnpike Trust.

G. Marl Farm has many interesting traditional buildings. The farmhouse seems to have been restyled in the Georgian period to give it a formal, 'civilised' appearance. In the early twentieth century, Thomas Owen ran the farm as a commercial dairy, supplying milk to Llandudno and the surrounding area.

H. Marl Hall may originally have been so named because of the prevalence of this type of clay soil. In the past marl was commonly extracted and spread on fields to improve the soil quality. The earliest reference to a house here is in 1616, when it was a dwelling of the Holland family of Conwy. In 1627 Marl was purchased by John Williams, a very significant figure in the history of North Wales. He was initially responsible for improving the fortifications of Conwy Castle on behalf of King Charles. When Charles subsequently refused to heed his advice not to over-tax the Welsh he switched sides, and actually took part in the Parliamentary assault on Conwy Castle in August 1646. Marl Hall was destroyed by fire around this time, possibly as a result of an act of the Civil War, but it was rebuilt in about 1661. Fire struck again in the early eighteenth century and the building lay in ruins, with just one wing habitable for more than a hundred years. Ownership of the Hall included the right to operate the Conwy Ferry and when Colonel Lloyd lived here (1818-35) he was said to have personally attended at the ferry. His interests were social rather than proprietorial as he was keen to spot 'geniuses and characters' to invite back to his mansion. By the time of the local Enclosure Act, 1843, Marl was owned by Thomas Williams of Beaumaris which gave him a place at the trough with the Mostyn's, but a far more modest meal of thirty acres of Llanrhos common and twenty-eight acres in Llandudno. About 1870 a Mr Henry Woodhall bought and began restoration work on the Hall. Around the turn of the century it became a women's convalescent home, operated by the Birmingham Hospitals Saturday Fund. It is now run as an Outdoor Centre by Warwickshire County Council.

7. Continue walking along the lane until you notice the lodge (I) on your left.

I. Marl Lodge may have been operated as a formal entry-control in its early years, as the main house was certainly grand enough to suggest such a relationship. The subsequent decline of the hall meant that by the early eighteenth century it was home to a series of agricultural labourers. With Woodhall's restoration work the status of the big house rose and the lodge provided a home for the assistant gamekeeper, Richard Roberts, prior to his engagement as gamekeeper at Pabo Hall.

8. Continue until you notice Narrow Lane branching off to the right. Cross to admire the extensive view over the valley, with the main features identified for you by an engraved interpretive plaque; (you might also find the benches provided here a useful facility). Before continuing, look behind you to the cliffs (J) behind Marl Hall.

J. A Roman Signal Station is thought to have existed at the top of these cliffs. No evidence remains on the ground but it is likely that this spot would have been used to monitor movements at the strategically important head of the Conwy Valley. Fires could have been lit to alert the fort at Caerhun.

9. Walk down Narrow Lane, but take the path which breaks off to the right before you reach the roundabout. Cross carefully, and take the path to the right. The path soon turns sharply to the left, and crosses a small residential road. Cross to the continuation of the footpath which passes the rear of an old disused building set in extensive grounds (K).

K. This was last known as Albini House when it operated as part of a fee paying Catholic School with its main campus in Rhos-on-Sea. Originally known as Nant-y-coed, in the early years of the century it had provided a private residence for solicitor Vincent Johnson. In the nineteen thirties it was briefly the home of Tan-y-bryn School, which had relocated from Llandudno. For many years it provided vacations for the faithful when it was administered by Yorkshire Christian Endeavour Holiday Homes Ltd.

10. Follow the footpath to the road, Ronald Avenue. Turn right and follow the road down to the main road, and our refreshment stop at Maelgwyn Tea Rooms (L).

L. MAELGWYN TEA ROOMS

Address: 174 Conwy Road, Llandudno Junction

Refreshments: All day breakfasts, sandwiches, cakes, baked potatoes and a good range of snacks, meals and drinks

Description: A wonderful, individual tea-room which also sells interesting secondhand books and curios. Previously a wet-fish shop, the owners have created a quirky, attractive, quiet oasis of civilised refreshment. The food and drink is all excellent value, and the service is personal and relaxed. One can only wonder why places like this are so rare, and McDonalds so common.

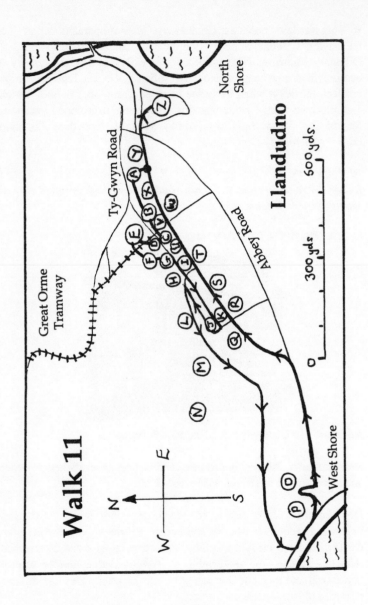

Walk 11

Llandudno

North Shore

West Shore

Ty-Gwyn Road

Abbey Road

Great Orme Tramway

300 yds.

500 yds.

Llandudno Village to Llandudno Town

Walk Number: Eleven

Distance: Two and a half miles

Terrain: Fairly easy, mainly level, paved surfaces

Start: Outside the Empire Hotel, Church Walks, Llandudno

Finish: Circular

Transport: Central location

Introduction:

In 1840, Llandudno was a mining village with some scattered agricultural smallholdings. There was a bit of fishing, and a few basic shops and inns. The population was around eight hundred and the community centred on the lower slopes of the Great Orme. Over the next twenty-five years mining ended but the population tripled. The new fashionable, sophisticated members of society were to be seen admiring the boutiques that had sprung up along Church Walks. Llandudno Village had become Llandudno Town. This walk maps out the Old Llandudno, and the New, and considers some of the social and economic forces that effected the transition.

The Walk and Points of Interest:

1. Walk down Tan yr Ogof Lane, to the left of the Empire Hotel. Begin to ascend the steps but pause half way up (A).

A. On the site that is now occupied by the hotel's swimming pool was a steam engine which pumped water from the mines. The water turned a fifteen foot diameter waterwheel, which powered an ore-crusher. The small houses above, in Tan yr Ogof Terrace also date back to the days of the old mining village.

2. Turn left along Tŷ Coch Road (B).

B. This quiet lane was a hive of activity in mining days. The Ty Gwyn Mine Company had their offices, smithy and carpenters shop here. The house on the right, half way along was the original Ty Coch Farmhouse, which gave its name to the lane. This was the home of Edward Owen who also ran a small butchers shop here. Ty Coch formerly had a high thorn hedge which sheltered the meetings of a group of local Mormons. Their claims met stiff opposition from the Scripturally well-versed miners. These lively exchanges often continued until ten or eleven at night. At one noted meeting, John Parry's claim to understand strange tongues was met with the less biblically inspired response that Parry could 'no more speak Greek than Ty'nfron's cow could knit socks'!

3. Continue to the end of the lane, and notice the tram station (C).

C. The Victoria Station got its name not directly from the queen but from the house that previously occupied the site. This was the home of George Brookes, the agent of the Ty Gwyn Mine.

4. Turn right and in a short distance you notice a pub (D) on your left.

D. The King's Head is credited with a key role in the transition of Llandudno. The notion of transforming a remote mining community into an elegant bathing resort is said to have been first discussed here. It struck a chord with the agent of Llandudno's foremost landowner, Lord Mostyn. He passed the idea to his master and, as you know, the rest is history . . .

Continuing up Old Road, and you soon notice some small houses (E) on your right.

E. Number 19, Old Road, was Mrs Ann Jones' village post office from about 1838. In those days, before postage stamps came into use, the receiver of letters had to pay the postage cost rather than the sender. The little houses in front of the old post office (now 19 and 20 Old

Road) were known as Tŷ Newydd Cottages in village days.

5. Retrace your steps a little and pause behind the King's Head (F).

F. This area used to be known as Tanyberllan, and it was the village square. Miners would sit on low walls and read newspapers, usually Yr Amserau; chat and generally meet each other. Old characters often enlivened the scene with their jokes and stories. Tom Parry was known for his ready wit whilst Owen Jones, the pig killer, had tales of fairies, ghosts and goblins.

6. Continue along Llwynon Gardens, but pause outside Caersalem Chapel (G).

G. The Caersalem Welsh Wesleyan Chapel opened in 1837 reminds us that Llandudno village was very much a Welsh speaking community. Incidentally, a plaque records that the chapel later served as a school which educated William Morris Hughes, a past Prime Minister of Australia. It does not record his shameful record of racism in promoting an apartheid 'Whites Only Australia', policy.

Continue along until the path forks in front of you (H).

H. The continuation of Llwynon Gardens becomes Cwlach Street and it is this lane that was the axis of the old village, with little shops and cottages and stables along its length. Some of the outbuildings at the rear of the houses on the left incorporate bits of earlier shops that faced onto the lane. Some of the houses that you will see on the right began life as modest miners' cottages. The character of the narrow lane itself provides a clue to its origins, as it follows the contour along the side of the hill.

7. Do not go up the hill, or down, but continue ahead past (I).

I. Tan-y-nant used to stand on the left. Marged Jones, who ran a bakehouse here, had an interesting way of communicating to customers that the baking was finished, and that fresh bread was available. She would clamber onto the wall in front of Tan-y-nant, and blow into a large seashell until it resounded like a trumpet.

Continue for one hundred yards or so until you notice a terrace of four small cottages (J), set back on the right, and a building (K) on the opposite side.

J. These houses have maintained much of their original character. The cottage at the end, on the right, was the home of the blacksmith at the Ty Gwyn Mine, Thomas Owen. Next door to him lived Ellen and Enoch Hughes, who made clogs for the miners. Ann and Owen Owens were next to them with Richard and Sarah Hughes, who sold flour, in the end house on the left hand side.

K. Catrin Parry's sweet shop was a part of the buildings opposite. Besides different coloured sticks of candy and mints she sold a range of animal shaped cakes, with currants for eyes. Her artistry was mocked by Thomas Rowlands who claimed that: 'It was too great a task for any philosopher to differentiate between the dog and the ass and between the pig and the ox.'

8. Continue to the end of the lane, and then ascend the steps on the right. Turn right and continue – you get a good overview of the layout of the old village. You soon join a paved road; pause here and look at the large houses (L) in front and to the left.

L. These grand houses are Victorian Villas of the new, planned Llandudno. Notice especially the famous black and white Tower House which betrays a rather Gothic influence, in contrast to the house next door. This is a cream coloured confection in the Italianate style, much favoured by Queen Victoria at Osborne House (1849) on the Isle of White. The chunky tower here is based on the 'campanile' of medieval Italian villas. The designs for these houses were suggested by the architects employed by Mostyn Estates. They were intended as a conscious contrast to the houses of the working class, such as those

116

immediately below you, which display none of this elegance or awareness of cosmopolitan influences.

9. Turn left and continue until you come to our refreshment stop at Haulfre Gardens (M).

M. HAULFRE GARDENS

Address: Cwlach Road, Great Orme, Llandudno, tel: 01492-876731

Refreshments: Tea, coffee, soft drinks, sandwiches, cakes and snacks

Description: This is an unmissable Llandudno experience. Personal service in an attractive, historic setting, with a unique view. The Haulfre Gardens were developed by Henry Pochin before he moved on to even grander schemes at Bodnant Gardens. In 1887 the present tearooms were built as a summer residence for the grocery magnate, Sir Thomas Lipton. In 1929 David Lloyd George, who was then the local M.P. formally opened the gardens to the public.

10. Whilst you rest and enjoy your refreshments you might care to consider further what was happening here in the mid-nineteenth century (N).

N. On the Orme the way of life had changed little over the years.

Mining, farming and a bit of fishing were the mainstays, with many people doing bits of each. Work, worship and social life were conducted in Welsh. On 25th April 1848 the rights of the ordinary residents of Llandudno to graze their animals, hold fairs or even walk on the commons were ended. They were legally stolen from them by the big landowners who designed, enacted and enforced the local enclosure act. Of the 955 acres over which they could previously legitimately exercise their rights they were henceforth permitted one and a half acres for a recreation ground, and thirty square yards for a well. Edward Mostyn, already the largest freeholder of land in the area, was awarded 832 acres of the commons to do with as he pleased. This was the very same Honourable Edward Mostyn Lloyd Mostyn, M.P. who had piloted 'The Eglwysrhos, Llandudno and Llangystennin Enclosure Bill' through parliament. Smallholders who held their land by tradition and convention rather than legal documentation lost not only grazing rights but their homes as well. About twenty families were evicted from the sea front area and their homes were demolished. In future their land would provide Mostyn Estates with premium income from prestige hotels. As opportunities for smallholding dramatically decreased, opportunities for mine work also began to disappear as the mines were closed down. The villagers of old Llandudno would just have to sink or swim in the new Llandudno Bathing Resort.

11. Continue your walk ahead through the gardens which have been recently restored. The wonderful views soon become even more extensive. Continue until you reach the West Shore and descend; turn left and walk along Abbey Road, and take the first left along Abbey Place. Continue and stop at the head of the stream (O); this is another very important mining site.

O. This stream comes from deep inside the old Orme copper mines. The tunnel, or adit, is half a mile long and was dug through solid rock by a team of twelve miners who worked in shifts, day and night for eight years until 14th October 1842. When the main body of water had disbursed, the miners laid tracks through the adit and wagoned out the ore through here. This area was also used for crushing and washing the ores, and for storage in large bins until it could be shipped out from the West Shore. Much of this processing of the ores was tedious manual work, that was carried out by children who earned about four old pence a day each.

12. Notice a house named Glan-y-don (P) nearby.

P. This was built about 1750 and was for many years a miner's cottage. At the end of its original garden was the smithy and carpenter's shop of the New Mine. It was here that the only ship ever built in Llandudno was constructed. It was the Sarah Lloyd, which was launched in 1863 and designed as a 'flat' to carry ore. It was named after the wife of David Lloyd, the master mariner who had leased the Old Mine in April 1861. Ironically he had missed the boat. Mining was in grave decline and his ship had to find employment elsewhere. A terrace of miners' cottages also existed nearby from about 1747, until they were demolished in 1936. One of these cottages was used as a dressing room when the Reverend Robert Roberts baptised people in the sea here, about 1800.

13. Return to Abbey Road and continue left until the road forks. Take the left hand fork, Church Walks, but keep to the right hand side of the road for the better view of the buildings. Notice Plas Brith (Q) on your left.

Q. Plas Brith represents the triumph of the new over the old. Previously the cottages of Tai Newyddion stood here; 'With pretty little gardens in front of them, which were neatly kept and full of fruit trees, and they and their occupants were a perfect picture of true happiness and a good neighbourhood.' Margaret and William Davis, 'The Shepherd' lived here. In the pre-enclosure days everyone was entitled to keep a few sheep on the common, and they paid William a small amount per head to shepherd them. The annual Great Orme Sheep Fair held on 22nd September was a big event in Old Llandudno, but the enclosure act ended all that. In 1849 Mostyn Estates parcelled up the old commons for leasehold sale and development. Plas Brith and the other sophisticated buildings along here are a result of that process. Between 1850 and 1860 Church Walks became the commercial and administrative centre of the new town.

Continue and you soon notice a school building (R).

R. St George's National School was built in 1846. It was opened under the aegis of the 'National Society of the Church of England' who promoted the building of 'National Schools', to 'Communicate to the poor . . . such knowledge and habits as are sufficient to guide them through life in their proper stations . . . and to train them to the performance of their religious duties . . . '

Continue to the church (S).

S. St George's Church was opened after the original parish church up on the Orme had been wrecked in the 1839 storm. The fact that this new, larger church was built and opened down here in 1840 but St Tudno's wasn't even repaired until 1855 demonstrates how the old village was on the way down and Llandudno Town was on its dynamic way up. St George's was officially appointed Llandudno parish church in 1862.

14. Crossing the end of Llewelyn Avenue you can see the Royal Hotel (T).

T. The Royal Hotel was the first major hotel to be built in Llandudno. Originally it was known as the Mostyn Arms, and opened with thirty-five beds.

15. On the left hand side, notice the crenellated building (U), while a little further along, again on the left, is 68 Bryn Arfon (V).

U. The Bodlondeb Castle was built as a home for the son of the founder and owner of St George's Hotel, Isaiah Davies, but it is said that he never actually lived there. It soon became Mrs Annie Eakin's School for the daughters of gentlemen. During the First World War it was used as a military hospital. Later, in 1931, it was taken over and continues to be used as a Methodist Holiday Hotel.

V. 68 Bryn Arfon was originally the headquarters of the Llandudno Water and Gas Company in 1856, vital for the development of the new town. A gas works was opened in 1857 and 40 gas street lamps were erected in 1860.

16. Cross the foot of Old Road and notice, on your right again, Ormeside Court (W).

W. This was originally The George and Dragon Inn, which was later replaced by Goulding's Private Hotel (see advert).

17. A little further along, on your left again is 70 'Capri' (X).

X. 70 Capri was the original 'Town Hall', being the home of Llandudno's Board of Improvement Commissioners from 1854 until 1902. The Chairman of the Board was the Honourable Thomas Edward Mostyn Lloyd Mostyn and the commissioners soon built up a considerable reputation for financial incompetence. Until his death in 1861 Thomas Mostyn attended five, of the more than two hundred and fifty, meetings of the two commissioners. 72 'Bella Vista', on the corner, was the town's first bank; a branch of the National Provincial, which was opened in 1866.

18. We return to our starting point at the Empire Hotel (Y), and a little further ahead, you will see the Parade Hotel (Z).

Y. The Empire Hotel was, from 1854, a sort of early supermarket; the Italian Warehouse. It was operated by Thomas Williams whose entrepreneurial talents also ran to writing an early guidebook promoting the town, a Complete Guide to Llandudno.

Z. The Parade Hotel retains its original name, but the Victoria was previously the 'Pier'. It is the rear of these buildings that is most interesting. The Parade has its old stables, and tucked away behind the Victoria is the original Llandudno Police Station.

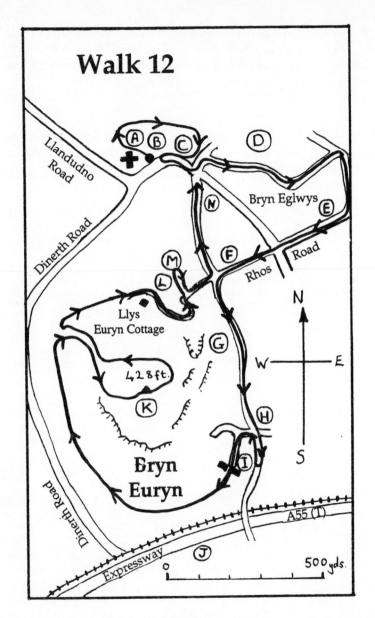

Walk 12

Llandudno Road

Dinerth Road

(A) (B) (C) (D)

Bryn Eglwys

(N) (E)

(F) Road

Rhos

(M)

(L)

Llys
Euryn Cottage

(G)

428 ft.

N

W — E

S

(K)

(H)

Bryn
Euryn

(I)

Dinerth Road

A55 (T)

Expressway

(J)

500 yds.

A Hillfort, a Mansion and a Church
with a Curious Tower

Walk Number: Twelve

Distance: Three miles

Terrain: Mostly fairly easy and level, but some rough woodland paths and a slightly strenuous ascent up Bryn Euryn.

Start: Llandrillo-yn-Rhos Church

Finish: Circular

Transport: Bus 12 & 15, four an hour

Introduction:

Penrhyn Bay and Rhos-on-Sea are largely recent developments but people have lived up here at Llandrillo-yn-Rhos for most of the last two thousand years, although the parish was known as Dinerth until 1540. The lower lying land towards the sea was marshy, with Afon Ganol snaking its way across on its way to the sea. Years ago Old Price wrote of, ' . . . a vast roadless marsh of reed, bulrushes and ponds, the haunt and breeding ground of countless waterfowl'. The church stood as a beacon for all around. Higher still is the original settlement on Bryn Euryn, which also stood guard over the ancient route which passes around its southern slopes. On the lower slopes of Bryn Euryn, Ednyfed Fychan, the Seneschal or stewart of Llewelyn Fawr, chose to build his medieval manor house.

The Walk and Points of Interest:

A. Ednyfed Fychan founded Llandrillo church, and his private chapel is thought to have been incorporated into the existing building. The church tower dates from 1552 although the very unusual stepped corner section was probably added fifty or so years later. This feature was designed to provide a lookout for the approach of pirates in the bay, and it is a link in a chain which includes the tower encountered in

Walk Fifteen. A brazier would be lit to provide a warning beacon to other signal towers along the chain. Before the over enthusiastic renovations of 1857 the ancient east window featured the coat of arms of Ednyfed Fychan. Only two fragments survive, and these are incorporated into the present vestry window. The new east window commemorates the recovery from illness of Edward Brookes of Pabo in 1873. The west window commemorates the controversial conductor Jules Rivière. There was a cause célèbre in 1827 when the church silver was stolen. The thief, Hugh Williams, was arrested, convicted and sentenced to transportation for seven years.

1. We start at the church (A), with its lychgate and churchyard (B), which was very favourably reviewed in Jackson's travel guide of 1861: 'What a snug sequestered spot, how favourable to repose and meditation'. Several specific features deserve attention.

B. The lychgate of 1677 is one of the oldest in the area. The sun-dial that is mounted on a column is even more unusual. The dial itself was stolen is 1998 but the inscription just under the rim can still be discerned. It reads, *Th. Ow(en), 1756.* The grave memorials extend back to the seventeenth century and exemplify the wide geographical area served by the Parish before the development of the nineteenth century resorts. Notice the monument to William Bostock of Plas Euryn, died 20.02,1895, who was responsible for the initial development of Rhos-on-Sea as a new bathing place; T.G. Osborn, died 07.04.1910, was the founder of Rydal School; but more intriguing is the 'Unknown Sailor'. A body was found floating off Rhos Point on the last day of 1894 wearing a life-belt inscribed 'Loweswater', and with a cross tattooed on his arm. The owners of the Loweswater, Jackson, Metcalfe & Co., of 14, Water Street, Liverpool were contacted and an inquest was organised. The owners claimed to know nothing of the man and refused to attend the inquest. The inquest jury denounced the owners, and all the jurors attended the funeral here as a last token of respect for a man whose identity remains a mystery to this day. Harold Lowe's name is known all round the world as an officer who played an heroic role in enabling at least some to escape the sinking of the Titanic. His grave is best found by entering the lower graveyard via the western gate. Turn left and walk down the path for about twenty-five yards; the grave is on the right next to the path.

2. Walk back to the car park, to the east of the church, and notice the very large house (C) adjacent.

C. This is the vicarage which dates from 1903 and is actually the third successive one known to have been built here. The best known incumbent was probably the Reverend William Venables Williams, M.A., Jesus College, Oxford. Vicar from 1869 until 1900, for those 31 years he was a cornerstone of local society. When the new purchaser of the Estate which was to be developed as Colwyn Bay first arrived, it was Venables Williams who headed the reception committee. When wealthy locals wanted the railway to pay higher rates so that they would be called on to contribute less, it was Venable Williams who successfully prosecuted their case. When impoverished local smallholders and farmers asked the church to renegotiate the rates (tithes) it demanded of them, it was Venables Williams who steadfastly refused. In response, his mission church in Colwyn Bay was burnt to the ground, though their threat to also blow up his vicarage was not carried out. Undaunted, he set about replacing his mission church with the present St Paul's Church in Colwyn Bay. He hoped to hold the new living of Colwyn Bay as well as Llandrillo. When the Bishop refused, the dispute became acrimonious; Venable Williams publicly expressed his bitterness to his parishioners, the House of Commons became involved and Venable Williams even wrote a personal letter to Queen Victoria, but the Bishop's view prevailed.

3. Leave the church grounds and turn left along Llandudno Road, left down Church Road, then right along Bryn Eglwys Road through the housing estate (D).

D. This Housing Estate was built between 1952 and 1956 and designed by Sidney Colwyn Foulkes, the foremost architect of Colwyn

Bay. I find it rather bland, with an unimaginative use of landscaping but Pevsner's guide calls it, 'One of the best of Colwyn Foulkes' many local authority housing schemes' with 'lighthearted porches' and 'delicate touches in glazing bars'.

4. Turn right up Rhos Road and pause outside the first two sets of semi-detached stone houses (E).

E. Notice the inscribed date stone which includes the letters W.D. The letters stand for Whitehall Dod, the Estate owner when these houses were built in 1857. They were built as houses to serve the Bryn Euryn quarries which we will see later. Numbers 56 and 58 were also built for Whitehall Dod in a similar style, but about thirty years later.

5. Continue up Rhos Road, cross at the lights and continue until you notice a range of much renovated stone buildings (F) on your right.

F. These are the old buildings, or rather facades, of Bryn Euryn Farm. Earlier in the century the farm was owned by Victor Wilde, a cotton and shipping magnate from Lancaster who sold off eighteen acres of the farmland to the Council in 1952 for the building of the Estate that we have just visited. (Did you notice Victor Wilde Drive?)

6. Turn left along Tan-y-bryn Road, which still retains a rural atmosphere, and continue to Bod Euryn (G).

G. Bod Euryn is typical of the large turn of the century houses that were built along here on the lower slopes of Bryn Euryn, but unlike most of the others it has survived. The fate of Tan-y-bryn, which previously stood next door, has sadly been more typical. It was bought by a property company who wanted to demolish and redevelop the land, but the council were reluctant to give permission. The local Civic Society wanted the building to be given statutory protection when suddenly in 1995 the building was destroyed in an arson attack. Modern houses have now been built on the site.

7. Continue until you come to Ebberston Road West on your left, notice the building behind the high wall (H).

H. This is an old Lodge cottage built circa 1860 by Whitehall Dod in his typical semi-gothic Estate style. Originally it controlled traffic along the lane which predated Ebberston Road, and led to a Bath House on the shore.

Continue along Tan-y-bryn Road until you notice an old water pump (I).

I. This old lane was previously an important thoroughfare, and this was a welcome watering place. The pump has survived but the smithy didn't.

8. Retrace your steps for about fifty yards, turning left into Horton Drive. Continue until you reach Dolphin Court, built on the site of Whitehall Dod's old home, Bryn Dinarth. Go through the gap between the two sets of garages, ignoring any illegal notices calculated to deter walkers because this is a public footpath. Pass into the woodland, trying to ignore the roar of traffic in the valley (J) to the left.

J. This valley was part of the route taken two thousand years ago by Roman legions on their way to punish the Druids of Ynys Môn for their support of the Gauls against Roman rule. In 61 A.D. Suetonius Paulinus reached this point with twelve thousand legionnaires, but suddenly came under fierce attack. His second in command, Sempronius, was killed, and this valley is now referred to as Nant Sempyr.

9. Continue on this rather lovely walk through the trees, turning right and circling the lower slopes of the hill-fort. Continue on a slightly rising route until you reach the west of the hill where you can take one of several steeper routes to the summit (K).

K. Overlooking low-lying ground in all directions, Bryn Euryn was an obvious site for an Iron Age hill-fort. The scrub vegetation covering much of the hill makes it difficult to identify the remaining evidence of successive inhabitants but it seems that this site was occupied from a few hundred years before the Romans until the middle ages. It may have been abandoned in favour of lower ground during more settled periods of Pax Romana, but would have been reoccupied by the social elite during the more turbulent times after the Roman departure. In the middle ages an area to the south of the summit, but within the outer enclosure, seems to have been run as a rabbit farm. Two pillow mounds have been identified, which were a sort of artificial rabbit warren, and it has been suggested that a nearby hut circle could have been the home of the medieval warrener.

10. Descend by any of the routes to the west but then continue to encircle and descend by the path to the north; you pass by a house, Llys Euryn Cottage, on your right and descend to an old abandoned quarry (L) with a car park alongside.

L. These quarries, developed in the 1840's, were connected to a quay sited at the old pierhead in Rhos by a tramway with horse-drawn trucks. Usually described as running along Rhos Road, the tramway actually ran behind the quarry houses we saw earlier. Residents of the quarry cottages have found numerous old horse shoes along the route. Quarrying finally ended in the nineteen twenties.

11. Continue past the car park and ascend the steps on the left. Take this path until it opens out at a ruined building (M).

M. This is Llys Euryn, the thirteenth century manor house of Ednyfed Fychan; although what can be seen above ground dates from the fifteenth century or later. This fits in with the story that Ednyfed's Hall was razed to the ground during Owain Glyndŵr's rising, in about 1409. Although 'Edward Fychan had in Wales diverse goodly houses' this was 'his chiefest manorhouse'. The massive chimney and fireplace indicate that this was a huge hall, used for dining and entertaining. The house passed into the ownership of the Conway family, and the last occupants left in the 18th century. Since then the house has gradually fallen into disrepair.

12. Return to the lower level near the car park; turn left, and emerge onto Tan-y-bryn. Turn left again and walk until you reach the Ship Inn (N).

N. THE SHIP INN

Address: 9, Llandudno Road, Llandrillo (tel. 01492-540198)

Refreshments: Good value bar food or restaurant meals

Description: An attractive pub built in the Estate style by Whitehall Dod, in 1873. The original Ship Inn, opened in 1736 by Robert Davies, stood between the vicarage and the church and was demolished when this one was built.

Walk 13

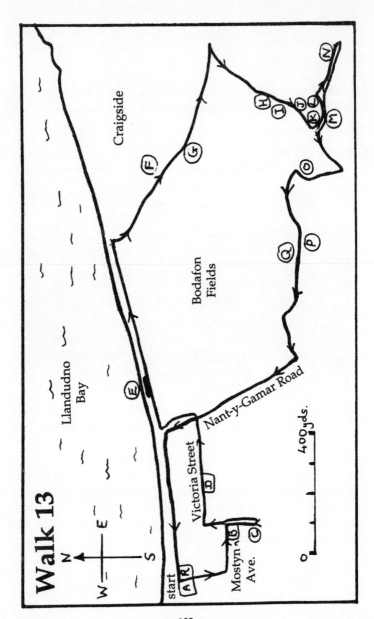

Bodafon and its Hidden Hamlet

Walk Number:	Thirteen
Distance:	Four miles
Terrain:	Good path surfaces but some steep slopes
Start:	Washington Hotel, East Parade, Llandudno
Finish:	Circular
Transport:	Centrally located

Introduction:

This walk explores three different areas. The first is Craig-y-don, the second Bodafon Fields, and the third is Pant y Wennol. Each area has a different history, which has resulted in distinct patterns of development. We begin in a commercial centre of shops, hotels and houses; continue along the only section of promenade that has not been commercially developed. We walk along a bridleway alongside farm fields and ascend to an old hamlet which has evidence of pre-Neolithic settlement. We look at a smallholding now completely abandoned before returning to the farmland now targeted for commercial development.

The Walk and Points of Interest:

A. This area is called Craig-y-don after the Ynys Môn home of Thomas Peers Williams who gained the freehold after the Enclosure Act. His ownership of the Marl Estate before the enclosures provided his voucher for claiming the freehold here. Unlike the Mostyns, Williams went for ready money and sold the building plots here with no leasehold restriction. Craig-y-don has consequently developed along different lines to much of the rest of Llandudno, which remains a Mostyn fiefdom. There is less uniformity of architectural design, and yet many of the buildings exhibit an attractive 'Arts and Craft' influence.

1. From the starting point (A), walk up Clarence Road, taking the first left along Mostyn Avenue, pause at the junction with Queen's Road (B).

B. The domed building on the corner here was Dunphy's high class grocery store. The shop was so well known that most people referred to this as Dunphy's Corner (and some still do). This is still the commercial heart of Craig-y-don although the area is not so much a separate community, distinct from Llandudno, as it was in the Edwardian era.

2. Take a look around the corner in Queen's Road, at the building next to the chapel (C).

C. This was a Livery Stable where horses could be left or rented. An essential facility for pre-internal combustion engine towns, such places have disappeared unnoticed from the landscape. Even the inscription, *Livery Stables, 1902* has gone from over the entrance. Its replacement, which advertised petrol, has also disappeared.

3. Turn back and walk down Queen's Road towards the sea, turning right into Victoria Street (D).

D. Victoria Street provided popular guest house accommodation for working class visitors whilst the more affluent could afford the elegance of the seafront hotels. Our main point of interest here, however, is the house-name of number 32, Tennis Court. This curious name relates to the courts of Messrs Riddell & Jarvis opened in 1885 on the land at the rear, which is now occupied by St Paul's Church.

4. Continue to the corner of Nant y Gamar Road, turn left to the sea-front, and continue to the right along the promenade, stopping at the paddling pool (E).

E. Plans were drawn up for this pool in 1936 because the pool at the West Shore was so monopolised by adults playing with their model yachts that the children couldn't get a look in.

5. Continue along the promenade until you see a road branching off to the right. Cross over and walk up Ffynnon Sadwrn Lane until you pass the houses on the left. Notice the spring on the green (F) to your left.

F. This is Ffynnon Sadwrn, named after Sadwrn, the brother of Illtud. In the nineteenth century this was much appreciated locally as a water supply. It was considered especially good for brewing beer. Land drainage is thought to have adversely affected the flow of water.

6. Continue straight on when the road turns to the left, and you should be on a very pleasant bridleway. Continue until you notice a gap (G) on the right.

G. This led to the tramway from Colwyn Bay to Llandudno which ran parallel to the lane here, before heading off across the fields. This gap lead to a small shelter and a sign announcing this as *Craigside Stop.*

7. Do not turn off, but continue to walk along the lane until you finally emerge at the corner of the fields where a house has been built at the point where the tram originally entered the fields. Turn right here along Bodafon Road, and you soon come to a small stone built school (H).

H. This is Bodafon Church of England School, which was opened under the sponsorship of Lady Augusta Mostyn on 18th April 1872. Her initials and motto are inscribed in stone above the main entrance. Until 1928 the building also served as Church Mission rooms. A very attractive gothic design was selected and the architect for both the school and the schoolhouse, next door, was George Felton of the Mostyn Estate.

8. Do not walk in front of the school but turn left and climb the steep road which passes behind it. Continue a little way until you see another building, built in a similarly Gothic style, below you (I).

I. This is Bodafon School House which was completed before the end of the 1872 academic year and immediately occupied by the first schoolmistress, Anne Selina Barker. The house is now privately occupied and no longer connected with the school, having been sold by Mostyn Estates in 1990.

9. Continue for about one hundred yards until you notice, but do not follow, a very overgrown path (J) going off sharply to your left. It seems to be going off into the cliff face.

J. This path does indeed lead into a cave. The cave was occupied in 1742, and for a good few years afterwards, by John Thomas who paid the Gloddaeth Estate four pence a year rent. Either John or a later tenant sought to improve living conditions by building a simple, single storey cottage in front of the cave, probably around 1760. The cottage continued to be occupied by various tenants for 150 years until it was left derelict, and then used only for storage. Now without a roof it looks forlorn but romantic.

10. Continue walking up the hill, and you soon come to group of cottages. The range to the left are difficult to identify, especially as separate cottages have latterly been combined to form single larger residences; but try to pick out an old stone house chimney to your left (K).

K. The house here was probably the first to be erected in this little settlement of Pant y Wennol. When John Thomas was shivering down below in his cave at fourpence a year, Robert Williams was up here luxuriating in his little cottage at four shillings a year. One resident who went on to gain fame of national proportions was born here on the 7th November 1821. Thomas Kendrick's father was a miner on the Great Orme, and initially he followed in his footsteps. Around 1845 he moved to live at Tan-yr-ogof on the Great Orme, and work in the copper mines. As mining ended and tourism began, he concentrated on lapidary work, and decided to dig out the cave in his garden to provide additional workshop space. He broke through much accumulated rubble and into the newspapers and record books, for he found four human skeletons and much other archaeological material that established beyond doubt that people had lived on the Orme since Neolithic times. The other buildings you can see here in Pant-y-Wennol were added in the nineteenth century to eventually form three little terraced blocks of ten separate houses.

11. Slightly higher up is a white painted, rather square looking, dwelling called Penberth (L).

L. Penberth was originally the chapel for Pant-y-wennol. Opened in 1861, it served this small community of mainly agricultural workers. When the larger Bethania Chapel opened in Craig-y-don in 1886, most of the chapel members preferred to worship there and the chapel here was converted into a house. Over the years there has been extensive remodelling, but it is just possible to discern the building's origins.

12. Walk slightly further uphill and notice the house ahead (M) and to the right.

M. Pant Uchaf has also been modernised almost out of all recognition, but if you concentrate on the single storey section on the right, you might be able to spot the mid-nineteenth century origins of the house.

13. Continue walking along the path, which turns to the left as it climbs gently higher. Soon, you see the tumbled ruins of a little cottage (N).

N. Though there is little left to see, it is interesting to realise that 'Mount Pleasant' was a family home until 1954. Frederick and Emma Hughes brought up their two daughters, Ruth and Megan, here. Whilst Llandudno town had all the trappings and comforts of civilisation well before the dawn of the twentieth century, Frederick, with his horse and cart, was carrying all life's necessities, including coal and water, up the hill to this cottage until he died in 1954. In many ways the old Pant-y-wennol died with Frederick. In the nineteenth century Pant-y-wennol was a community of about seventy people, living in fourteen separate houses; in the late twentieth century there are only four occupied houses.

14. Walk back down the hill to point L. Now your way lies down to the left, along by the wall. Continue on this path passing above and around the ground of a large house (O).

O. Built as Bryn Glas in the 1880s in an acre or so of land, the name was soon changed to the present one of Eryl Fryn. The property was initially a private residence run by a domestic staff of nine. The building in the grounds (now unconnected) was built as a lodge and coach house about 1900. In recent years Eryl Fryn has been enlarged and converted into a residential nursing home.

15. Turn left and continue until you come to two substantial ranges of buildings. Notice the one on the left (P) and the one on the right (Q).

P. Bodafon Hall was the original Bodafon farmhouse, with the present farmhouse being a conversion from part of the original range of agricultural buildings. The present 'Hall' dates mainly from the 18th century, with the coach house and servants' quarters at the rear dating from 1820 to 1840. Many of the occupants of the small cottages dotted hereabouts would have found work on what was originally an arable farm of around one hundred acres. An interesting entry in the Llandudno parish registers of 1817 records the birth of an illegitimate child 'in the woman's abode at Bodafon'. The best known tenant was John Williams, who moved here in 1849. John Williams was the man who, as land agent for the Mostyns, was the person most responsible for drawing up the plans for the development of the town of Llandudno after the passing of the enclosure act. He wrote Llandudno's first tourist guide book to promote the town; he was secretary of the Tŷ Gwyn Copper Mining Company; Deputy Constable of Conwy; Churchwarded of St Tudno's; Clerk to the Llandudno Board of Improvement Commissioners; and in his spare time farmer at Bodafon! From 1882 to 1888 the Hall was occupied by Mrs Ann Jane Felton and her daughters. Jane Felton was the widow of George, who had earlier designed Bodafon school. From 1913 to 1922 the Hall was used as the Mostyn Estate Office. From 1922 until 1987 it was leased to a variety of tenants, who used it mainly as a hotel or guesthouse. In 1987 the freehold was sold and the Hall became a private house.

Q. Bodafon Farmhouse existed as a separate dwelling from about 1876, when it was created by Evan Jones from the centre wing of the existing (see above) Bodafon Farm buildings, which themselves were probably built between 1810 and 1820. Evan Jones also had another string to his bow as the pioneer of coach trips around the area. The Farm and the Hall continued to be part of the same holding but the Hall was sub-let until it was finally separated completely in 1913. Gradually the use of the farmland has moved from mainly arable to a greater concentration on dairying, with various plans in recent years for an altogether more commercial use.

16. Continue along Bodafon Road, turning right down Nant y Gamar Road, and left at the promenade to return to the Washington Hotel (R).

R. WASHINGTON HOTEL

Address: East Parade, Llandudno (01492-877974)

Refreshments: Good range of food but the beer on offer is less satisfactory.

Description: The Washington is a striking seafront building. Its exterior owes more to cinema design than the classic Victoriana of Llandudno's other seafront hotels. The explanation lies in the

Washington's history. It was originally developed from two houses that had been built here in 1854. Later developments along the front chose a building line set fifty feet further back from the sea, leaving The Washington standing out like a sore thumb. As motor traffic increased, the hotel's situation attracted criticism on traffic visibility grounds as well as for aesthetic reasons. The then owners, *Ind Coope,* finally succumbed to pressure and demolished the old building in 1924. The splendid new hotel we see today opened in April 1925. The occasion was marked by a game of billiards played between Llandudno and Colwyn Bay Councils; Llandudno were the victors.

Armed Troops and Popular Protest in Mochdre

Walk Number:	Fourteen
Distance:	Three miles
Terrain:	Rather hilly, some rough field tracks and thick undergrowth
Start:	The bridge over the railway, Station Road, Mochdre
Finish:	Circular
Transport:	Bus number 26, two per hour

Introduction:

The tithe was theoretically a farm tax of one tenth of produce paid annually to the Church. In practice, it had been commuted to a cash charge with much of the benefit going to rich landowners rather than poor clerics. In Victorian Mochdre, as in the rest of Wales, farm incomes were falling and poverty was widespread. Most local farmers were non-conformists who had no desire to hand over hard-earned cash to support the Established Anglican Church. They petitioned to get the tithe reduced but failed, and in 1886 a number simply refused to pay. Formal notices were sent out warning local farmers that bailiffs would seize goods if the tithes were not paid. In Mochdre, some farmers stood firm and the village prepared to resist . . .

The Walk and Points of Interest:

A. At 1.30 p.m. on 16th June 1887 a special train stopped on the track below you. Seventy-six police and seventy-six troops in 'heavy marching order, with a full supply of ball cartridge' alighted. Led by Major Hare, Lieutenant Tucker and the Chief Constables of both Denbighshire and Flintshire, they were to provide an escort for a distraining party of Church agents, court officials and an auctioneer. They were determined to collect the outstanding tithes, or seize goods in lieu. They were expected. Mochdre had prepared. Signal flags were

141

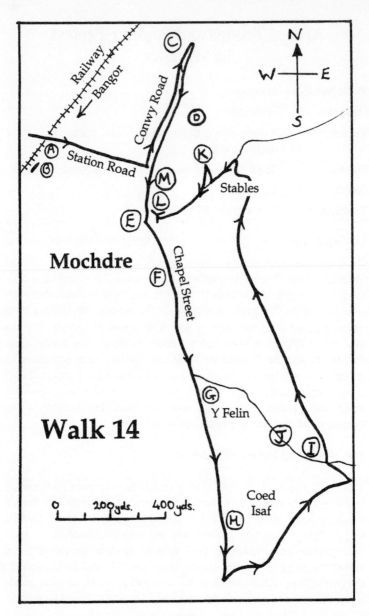

Railway
Bangor
Conwy Road
Ⓒ
Ⓓ
Ⓚ
Ⓐ
Ⓖ
Station Road
Ⓜ
Ⓛ
Stables
Ⓔ
Mochdre
Ⓕ
Chapel Street
Ⓖ
Y Felin
Ⓙ
Ⓘ
Walk 14
Coed
Isaf
Ⓗ

N
W — E
S

0   200 yds.   400 yds.

immediately run up poles on surrounding hills (the site of one is maintained at 'The Flagstaff', Colwyn Bay Zoo). Horns were blown, guns were fired and protesters rapidly gathered in the village. The bright red uniforms of the Cheshires marched off towards the inevitable confrontation . . .

1. We are standing on the bridge over the railway (A) on Station Road. Before you move off in the footsteps of the troops, it is interesting to note that the railway below (B) you is a historic spot in its own right.

B. This line opened as part of the Chester to Bangor Railway in 1848, and from the beginning the race was on to deliver the Irish Mail as quickly as possible. The need for steam engines to stop to take on water was one continuing source of delay. The Company Engineer, John Ramsbottom, eventually came up with a device which allowed trains to scoop up water from special troughs, whilst still on the move. It was here, below you, that the system received its successful world premier. The troughs were moved further along the line in 1871 and, unfortunately, the A55 ensured that all remains are now obliterated along with those of 'Mochdre and Pabo Station' (1889-1931). In 1887 there was no station; the train made a special stop and the police and troops jumped down onto the track.

2. Walk down Station Road towards the village (the service road running down to the right used to serve the station). Continue ahead until you reach the main Conwy Road. The forces of law and order marched on to the village, but let us take a short side trip here to visit the homes of two of those who still refused to pay. Turn left and continue for about three hundred yards until you reach a limestone boundary wall with two large upright stone pillars (C) (opposite 309 Conwy Road).

C. These are the gateposts, and all that remains, of Glan-y-wern Farm. Owen and Elen Pritchard lived here with their six children and grandchildren. Owen was one of the first tenants to withhold his tithe payment. On this fateful day he was going to be the last to receive his visit from the military.

3. Cross the busy main road and walk back about one hundred and fifty years towards the village centre. Between the car sales yard and number 351 you will notice a lane that is guarded by ornate metal gates. Do not go through, but walk on for a few yards for a better view of the house (D).

D. Tucked away from modern Mochdre is a remarkable survivor. Tan-yr-allt Isaf is an 18th century farmhouse which retains much of its original character. In 1887 it was the home of another tithe refuser who would soon be receiving his visit from the distraining party. The tenants here were John and Catherine Davies who, like the Pritchards at Glan-y-wern, spoke only Welsh.

4. Now it's time to catch up with the soldiery as they march onwards towards their first objective. Keep walking until you arrive back at the junction with Station Road. Just ahead of you, on your left, take the Old Conwy Road. Continue along here until you reach the pub (E).

E. This was the heart of the old village, with Tanrallt Street branching off to the left and Chapel Street to the right. On that 16th day of June, crowded into these narrow streets were about two hundred and fifty local people, gathered to demonstrate to the militia exactly what they thought of them and the unjust system that they had come to enforce. Booed, hissed, jostled and shouted at, the men in uniform with their motley collection of officials proceeded with some difficulty along Chapel Street.

5. Follow the troops along Chapel Street, and notice the severe beauty of the stone chapel (F) on your right.

F. This chapel was used as a meeting place in planning the anti-tithe campaign. One of the chapel deacons was Elias Hughes, one of the

144

most influential figures in the Mochdre anti-tithe movement (more of him later . . .).

6. Continuing along Chapel Street we seem a world away from the modern face of Mochdre. The scene was less peaceful as the villagers harried the Chief Constables' party every inch of the way; but this was as nothing compared to the scene awaiting them at the old mill. Continue until you arrive at the mill; where the road forks (G).

G. At this prearranged place were lines of farmers armed with five foot long wooden poles, and their ranks were being constantly swelled by others coming down from surrounding farms and villages. Some of the leaders of the official Anti-Tithe League appealed to the crowd for calm, but the general mood was for no surrender. The people were determined to stop any attempt to enforce payment or to distrain goods. The authorities had decided to move first against Hugh Roberts of Mynydd Farm. They somehow managed to force a way along the left hand fork and continue up the hill, with the by now huge 'unruly mob' brandishing weapons as well as insults.

7. At this point we briefly leave the action and take the opposite (right hand) fork in the road, to visit the home of another prominent protester. Continue along this lane for about four hundred yards, until you reach an old farm called Graianllyn (H).

H. Graianllyn is a mid-18th century farmhouse with a 17th century cruck barn. In 1887 it was the home of Isaac Morris who we shall now follow as he makes his way across to the home of his neighbour Hugh Roberts.

8. Continue along the lane, and soon it bends left over a little stream, which was traditionally used at this point as a sheepwash. Follow the paved lane around another bend, and notice a stile ahead as the lane turns uphill to the right. Cross this stile, and after fifty yards cross a ladder stile. Keeping a hedge on your right, continue over more stiles until you drop down into an enchanting small valley. Cross a little wooden bridge and bear left up a delightful lightly wooded path; you soon emerge onto a paved lane. Notice the old farmstead on your left (I).

I. This is Hugh Roberts' old Mynydd Farm. here we rejoin the action and the noise is deafening . . . Chief Constable Peter Browne of Flintshire and Chief Constable Leadbetter of Denbighshire had instructed twenty-six policemen to requisition some of farmer Roberts' stock, so that they could have an auction to pay off his tithe bill. Five hundred local people had other ideas. Whilst Major Leadbetter tried to placate them, angry anti-tithers questioned his authority and just 'made fun of him'. About one hundred farmers armed with sticks blocked the way of the twenty-six policemen. A brawl developed with more police, and even more protesters, joining the fray. When it seemed that the police were about to draw their truncheons to clear the lane, a group of onlookers decided to thwart their efforts with a hail of stones. This moved the battle into top gear. The police made wild attacks on the crowd, lashing out with their batons. The protesters no longer confined themselves to throwing stones and eggs, but added sharpened sticks and slingshot; one was alleged to have made a mounted charge into police ranks. Demands for 'Home Rule' were shouted and for several minutes the scene resembled a battle. Thirty-four police were injured and Major Leadbetter himself was struck and 'plastered all over the head with cow dung'. About fifty protesters were injured, some very seriously. Elias Hughes, the chapel deacon, had his 'skull . . . cracked and his arm broken' by the police. Isaac Morris of Graianllyn, who was said to be 'a very peaceably disposed man', was nevertheless also attacked by the police and injured. Seventy year old Hugh Roberts of Mynydd was left in a 'pitiful state'. He had been having an 'after-dinner nap' when the military and police arrived. His wife, who had been ill for two years was also in bed. Their servant knocked on their door and announced, 'They have come at last'. He went out, and after some preliminary discussions with Major Leadbetter a policeman jumped over the hedge and hit him over the head with his truncheon, knocking him to the ground. When his son arrived from Colwyn Bay and remonstrated with the police, he was told, 'You shall have it as well you devil'.

9. Before moving on, look down the paved lane (J) below Mynydd.

J. This leads down to Y Felin, and was the route taken by the troops on their way up here from the village, and the injured on their way down to be treated at Y Felin. Daniel and Grace Lloyd of Y Felin, did their best to bathe and repair the wounds of the injured farmers, and their home was reported as being 'awash with blood'.

10. Do not descend the lane as we are going to visit the home of William Jones, who had decided that it might be easier to pay up after all. We shall follow as he walks home to collect his money . . . Look for a footpath at the upper end of Mynydd Farm; it is signposted. Cross the stile and take the path to the left which goes up a short slope. You soon level out and continue along the same contour, under the same telegraph wires, for three quarters of a mile. The views along here are stunning, but towards the end the path can get a bit overgrown. When the wires eventually turn right look ahead, but slightly to the right, for a wooden pole with a curious metal arrow at the top. When you reach it, cross a couple of stiles, and turn left through the paddock. Go left again to the end of the stables, and then right, down the sunken lane that emerges onto a paved road. Here, you turn left and descend for about one hundred yards, where you notice Mere Rise on your right. Walk down here for a few yards and you will notice, amongst an array of modern houses, a beautifully restored old farmhouse (K).

K. This is Tan-yr-allt Ucha, the home of William Jones who was a 64 year old widower. He was making his way here when he was approached by a policeman. William explained that he was just on his way home to collect his tithe payment. The policeman, David Powell of Trefnant, replied by hitting him repeatedly on the head and arms, whereupon he fell insensible to the ground. More fighting broke out and the authorities decided to read out the riot act. It was translated into Welsh by Sergeant Lewis. Slowly the villagers dispersed and the authorities withdrew.

11. Return to Tanrallt Street, turn right and continue to walk down the road until you arrive, once again, at The Mountain View Inn, (see details). Over your refreshments you might wish to consider the outcome of that dramatic day's events.

L. Events that day in Mochdre were reported in the National Press and discussed both in Parliament and abroad. The anti-tithe struggles had led people in Wales to see a common cause with Nationalist struggles in Ireland. This was not lost on the authorities who were keen to contain and control the protests, now that outright repression had been seen to fail. They eventually managed to extract their tithe payments at Mochdre through distraint sales, but the ensuing public enquiry proved rather embarrassing for the authorities. The police were generally blamed for the violence, and when officers turned up at the enquiry in plain clothes it was suggested that this was a ploy to make it difficult for witnesses to identify them from their badge numbers. Even the policeman who had read the riot act (in Welsh), Sergeant Lewis of Abergele, was identified as having used unnecessary violence. It was claimed that he had pulled Edward Davies to the ground by his whiskers, whilst his police colleagues administered a beating with their staffs.

Public opinion remained firmly on the side of the protesters. The Mochdre tithe battle was a crucial event in a war which pushed the government towards reform. The eventual result was the disestablishment of the Church in Wales and the transfer of the responsibility for tithe payments for tenants to landlords. Where petitions and pleading had failed, direct action had succeeded.

M. THE MOUNTAIN VIEW INN

Address: Old Conwy Road, Mochdre (01492-544724)

Refreshments: Imaginative range of snacks and bar meals.

Description: This was also the village pub in 1887 when it was known as the White Horse and run by a sixty year old widow called Jane Davies. The name change came around the end of the century, probably to make it sound more attractive to the growing tourist market, who could now arrive via the newly installed railway station. Notice the old photographs of the village displayed on the walls of the lounge bar.

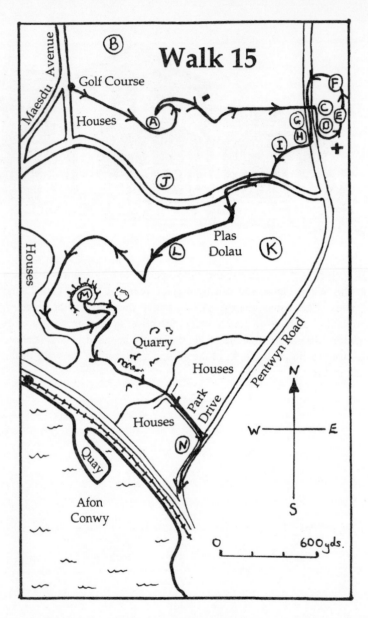

Walk 15

Maesdu Avenue

Ⓑ

Golf Course

Houses

Ⓐ

Ⓕ
Ⓒ
Ⓔ
Ⓖ
Ⓓ
Ⓗ
Ⓘ

＋

Ⓙ

Plas
Dolau

Ⓚ

Houses

Ⓛ

Ⓜ

Quarry

Houses

Pentwyn Road

Park Drive

N

W ────── E

Houses

Ⓝ

Quay

S

Afon
Conwy

O ──────── 600 yds.

Llanrhos and the Vardre

Walk Number:	Fifteen
Distance:	Three miles
Terrain:	Across fields with some moderate uphill sections
Start:	The intersection of Maesdu Avenue and Bryn Gosol Road
Finish:	Deganwy end of Pentwyn Road
Transport:	Frequent buses from Llandudno, 12, 14, 15, 16, 19

Introduction:

This walk takes in two of the most historic sites in the Llandudno area. Both are said to have been founded in the sixth century by Maelgwn Gwynedd, and both have a fascinating story to tell. The countryside in between is surprisingly picturesque, with numerous places of historic interest along the way.

The Walk and Points of Interest:

1. Cross the stile and take the footpath which passes behind the houses. Continue to the last house, cross the stile to the right and continue through the woodland. After two hundred yards, you emerge into more open, scrubby countryside, where you curve round to the left skirting the lower edge of the hill. After another couple of hundred yards, you ascend the northern slope of the hill to the tower (A).

A. This tower has been mistakenly described as both an outpost of Deganwy Castle and a windmill. Its construction details, and position, demonstrate its true role as part of a chain of watch towers stretching along the coast of North Wales. Constructed in the latter part of the sixteenth century, their allotted task was to identify any threat to local shipping posed by pirates offshore. Communication of the arrival of such a danger along the chain, and to the surrounding countryside, was accomplished by igniting beacon fires.

2. There are wonderful panoramic views from here; if you look towards Llandudno, you should notice a set of traditional farm buildings incongruously set in the middle of a local authority housing estate (B).

B. This is Cwm Howard Farm which, in part, dates from the sixteenth century. The outbuildings are later. The cartshed, with loft over, is probably late eighteenth century.

3. Descend by retracing your steps to the open land behind Bryniau Farm. Do not enter the farmyard, but cross the ladder stile. Cross the corner of the next field, over the stile and then follow the path down to the main Conwy Road. Cross to the corner of the churchyard. Do not enter yet, but notice a triangular area (C).

C. Notice that this roughly triangular area is walled off from the rest of the churchyard, and all the graves here are comparatively modern. In the nineteenth century this was the site of a public house, The Queen's Head. On the other side of the church, opposite the lychgate, was another larger pub with tennis courts and its own tea garden; the Mostyn Arms. Unfortunately Lady Augusta Mostyn didn't consider this arrangement conducive to worship, and in an act of characteristic Victorian benefaction had both inns pulled down.

4. Turn right and walk to the main lychgate entrance to the churchyard (D).

D. This is Llanrhos Church, dedicated to St Hilary and founded in the sixth century by Maelgwn Gwynedd. He is thought to have perished here, a victim of 'the yellow plague'. In the twelfth century a group of monks from Strata Florida settled here, possibly at Bryniau, and rededicated the church to St Mary. They moved on to Aberconwy Abbey when it was gifted to them by Llywelyn Fawr. The church was radically overmodernised in the nineteenth century but retains much of its earlier structure, especially its impressive main roof beams. Inside there are the family vaults of the Mostyns of Gloddaeth and the

Wynnes of Bodysgallen. The intriguing sixth century Christian memorial, the Tyddyn Holland Stone is also housed here. Before it was removed from Bodafon in 1908 the tenant of a nearby cottage, 'undertook to deepen the letters for the benefit of English tourists'. Other notable features are the eighteenth century lychgate; the mounting block next to it; and the memorial drinking fountain behind you, across the car park. Notice the fountain's inscription, denoting the connection of Llanrhos to the Llandudno water main in 1898.

5. Now have a wander around the graveyard and look out for the notable memorials (E).

E. A small plain headstone, slightly north of the church, tells a touching story; 'Here lieth the body of poor Betty who for upwards of 50 years was a houseless wandering maniac, died February 1824. Y mae gorphwysfa yn y Nefoedd.'

There are three memorials relating to Llanrhos institutions that no longer operate; Elizabeth Hughes of the old Post Office (north of the Church); John Hughes of the Queen's Head, and the Williamses who taught at Llanrhos School (both east).

A white upright memorial (north-east) with a dove perched on top of it records the grave of Cicianto Ferrari, the Llandudno Birdman. At the beginning of the century his performing bird show was a favourite of postcard and pier.

6. Now pass the railed-off Mostyn Section, and exit through the north-eastern gate nearby. Bear round to the left and you will see a black and white building in front of you (F).

F. This is one of the lodges to Gloddaeth Hall, one of the seats of the Mostyns. This was erected at the end of the nineteenth century, and has the family motto ostentatiously displayed above the window; Heb Dduw heb ddim, Duw a digon (Without God without anything, with God plenty).

7. Continue past the lodge to the main road and cross over again. Walk over to another attractive black and white building (G).

G. This building was erected on the instructions of Lady Augusta to provide suitable refreshment for the churchgoers of Llanrhos. It opened as a temperance hotel, popularly known as *The Cocoa Rooms,* in 1908. It was not a whirlwind success and today we must return to the fleshpots of Deganwy for refreshment, for Llanrhos no longer offers travellers ale, tennis, or even cocoa.

8. Continue to the next old stone building (H).

H. This opened in 1822 as a school. As part of the government's scheme of inspecting all schools in Wales, it received a visit from John James in 1847. There were only twenty-two children present in a building designed for eighty pupils. The walls were dirty and everything was covered in dust. The master apparently attempted to keep order by blowing a whistle every four minutes but this proved to have a rapidly diminishing effect. Only three pupils could read properly. A dreadful picture, but typical of the contemptuous tone adopted in most of these reports. They were considered biased, and were widely resented in Wales.

9. Walk down Cae Môr and continue along the footpath, notice the well (I) to your right in a private garden.

I. This used to be the principal water supply before the mains connection in 1898. It is quite likely that the church and original settlement was sited here because of the presence of this fresh water supply.

10. Continue to Bryn Lupus Road where you turn right and continue for a couple of hundred yards. Cross to the entrance to Plas Dolau, and from here you can look back at the tower we inspected earlier. Just in front of it is Plas Mariandir (J).

J. Opened in September 1919, Plas Mariandir was built for the Manchester and Salford Hospital Saturday and Convalescent Homes

Fund. This was not a charity but a co-operative association. Members qualified to use this facility by making thirteen weekly contributions of a penny. It was noted in the opening ceremony that, 'The new home would confer untold benefits upon the working people of Manchester and Salford, who in time of need would be able to leave the smoky city for a sojourn in pure air and sunlight.'

11. Continue down the drive to Plas Dolau, and where it turns right, glance ahead. In the near distance, slightly to the left, you can see (K).

K. Tyn-y-coed was built in 1878 for a Liverpool timber merchant called Davis. When he died in 1891 it was bought by the Birmingham Hospital Saturday Fund and run in a similar way to Plas Mariandir. In 1969 Tyn-y-coed was purchased by Robertson Research, an internationally important geological survey company.

12. Turn right, pass alongside the farm outbuilding, and continue along the lane (L).

L. Notice how the lane is sunken below the level of the banks on either side. Such paths are ancient landscape features known as holloways, and are due to the erosive effect of traffic through the ages. You are now walking in the footsteps of countless early travellers or villagers, who were also making for the Vardre.

13. Cross a stile, continue across the field, and go right after the next stile. Following the line of the fence, after the third stile follow the fence on the left this time. Pass the shelter sheds away to your left and continue around with the ruins of the castle, up on the hill to your left. When you reach the far side, follow the slope up to the top of the castle hill (M).

M. Deganwy Castle was raised by Maelgwn Gwynedd in the sixth century to guard Afon Conwy, which formed the eastern border of the Welsh heartland of Gwynedd. In the ninth century the castle was captured by the Saxons, who destroyed it. Over the next four centuries, when the Welsh were doing well, the border moved across the river to encompass the castle here. When the English were ascendant the Welsh retreated to their heartland. Consequently, Deganwy Castle was constantly being fortified and then destroyed by one side or the other. The existing, visible castle owes much to Henry the Third's building of around 1250, and its ruinous nature owes much to Llywelyn ap Gruffudd's destruction of 1263.

14. Descend to the gatehouse sign and continue to the stile. Make for the gap between the two hillocks, and you soon pass a kissing gate. Continue over a stile, and passing close to an old quarry, you soon exit through another kissing gate onto Park Drive. Continue ahead to Pentwyn Road, where you turn right and soon arrive at the Farmers Arms (N).

N. THE FARMERS ARMS

Address: Pentwyn Road, Deganwy (tel. 01492-583197)

Refreshments: Good range of bar meals

Description: A nice, quiet, characterful Victorian local.

Bibliography

Aris, Mary, *Historic Landscapes of the Great Orme* (1996).

Davies, H.R., *The Conwy and Menai Ferries* (1942).

Dibble, Kenneth, *Nant-y-Gamar* (1990).

Dibble, Kenneth, *Bodafon and Pant-y-wennol* (1993).

Dibble, Kenneth, *Rhiwledyn and Little Orme* (1995).

Dodd, A.H., *The Industrial Revolution in North Wales* (1933).

Forde-Johnston, J., *Hill-forts* (1976).

Hicklin, *Llandudno and its Vicinity* (1856).

Jenkins, Philip, *A History of Modern Wales* (1992).

Jones, Anthony, *Welsh Chapels* (1996).

Jones, Tim, *Rioting in N.E. Wales 1536-1918* (1997).

Lovering, John, *Gwynedd – A County in Crisis* (1983).

Lynch, Frances, *Guide to Ancient and Historic Gwynedd* (1995).

Parry, Tom, *Llys Helig* (1996).

Price, Geoff, *Llandudno and Colwyn Bay Trams* (1997).

R.C.A.H.M., *Inventory of the Ancient Monuments in Caernarvonshire 1: East* (1956).

Roberts, Jim, *Llandudno in Old Photographs* (1997).

Rowlands, Thomas, *Atgofion Hen Llandudno* (1883).

Senior, Michael, *The Crossing of the Conwy* (1991).

Sloan, Roy, *Early Aviation in North Wales* (1989).

Stamp, A.H., *Penrhyn Bay* (1996).

Taylor, Christopher, *Roads and Tracks of Britain* (1979).

Williams, C.J., *Great Orme Mines* (1995).

Williams, F. Ron, *Llandudno and the Mostyn Influence* (1996).

Williams, T., *Complete Guide to Llandudno* (1864).

Wynne Jones, Ivor, *Llandudno – Queen of Welsh Resorts* (1975).

Further Information

Llandudno Library – Local history collection includes directories, old maps, books, illustrations, census materials etc. for reference only (Mostyn Street, Llandudno, tel. 01492-574010).

Llandudno Museum – Artefacts, displays etc. depicting the history of the town (17-19 Gloddaeth Street, tel. 01492-876517).

Gwynedd Archive – A vast collection of original manuscripts, maps, Estate Papers etc. relating to the old county of Caernarfonshire of which Llandudno was a part (Victoria Dock, Caernarfon, tel. 01286-679095).

Mostyn Estate Office – A private collection of Estate Papers, plans etc., access is usually granted to bona fide researchers (Mostyn House, Llandudno, tel. 01492-876977).

Acknowledgements

This book could not have been produced without the help and support of many other people. It is impossible to acknowledge every contribution but I would like to take this opportunity to thank the staff of each of the above facilities as well as the following; Enid Powell of Bryn Pydew, Anna Jeffery of Penrhyn Bay, Tom Parry of The Great Orme Exploration Society, Graham Roberts of Rhos-on-Sea, Glenda Watson ex Bryn Pydew, Mona Williams of Henryd, Doris Morris of Glanwydden, David Birch of Rhos-on-Sea, John and Dorothy Owen of Bryn Pydew, Myrddin ap Dafydd of Carreg Gwalch and especially Neil Coombs of Colwyn Bay for the modern illustrations.

Index

WALKS IN WALES - latest titles

Walks from Llandudno
CHRISTOPHER DRAPER
ISBN: 0-86381-559-6; £4.95

Circular Walks in Meirionnydd
DOROTHY HAMILTON
ISBN: 0-86381-545-6; £4.50

Walks in and around the Berwyn Mountains
JOHN TRANTER
ISBN: 0-86381-547-2; £4.50

Circular Walks in North Eastern Wales
JIM GRINDLE
ISBN: 0-86381-550-2; £4.50

The North Wales Path and 10 selected walks
DAVE SALTER & DAVE WORRALL
ISBN: 0-86381-546-4; £4.50

Llŷn Peninsula Coastal Walks
RICHARD QUINN
ISBN: 0-86381-574-X; £4.50

Circular Walks in the Black Mountains
NICK JENKINS
ISBN: 0-86381-558-8; £4.50

Walks in the Wye Valley
RICHARD SALE
ISBN: 0-86381-555-3; £4.50